Cornwall

40 Coast & Country Walks

The author and publisher have made every effort to ensure that the information in this publication is accurate, and accept no responsibility whatsoever for any loss, injury or inconvenience experienced by any person or persons whilst using this book.

published by
pocket mountains ltd
The Old Church, Annanside,
Moffat, DG10 9HB
pocketmountains.com

ISBN: 978-1-907025-426

A catalogue record for this book is available from the British Library

Contains Ordnance Survey data © Crown copyright and database right 2014, supported by out of copyright mapping from 1945-1961

Printed in Poland

Introduction

Cornwall's extraordinary landscape has inspired generations of artists and writers, including Dylan Thomas, Sir John Betjeman, Daphne du Maurier, Barbara Hepworth and Stanhope Forbes.

And it's easy to see why – its rugged shoreline, sandy beaches, turquoise waters, meandering rivers, attractive woodland and open countryside combine to form one of the UK's most beautiful regions.

The diversity of landscape along its 700km of mainland coastline also makes Cornwall one of the best places for walking. Whether you're venturing into the lonely southeast corner of the Rame Peninsula; visiting beautiful towns and villages such as Fowey, St Ives and Padstow; enjoying the softer fringes of the Camel Estuary; experiencing the great cliffs of Cornwall's northern coast; discovering the rugged joys of the Lizard Peninsula or gazing across a vast expanse of sea as you reach Land's End, there are few better places to explore. Add to this an array of flora and fauna, some significant geology, striking architecture, and a history that extends back many thousands of years and you have the perfect walking destination.

History

Many of the cliffs along the Cornish coast are between 250 and 500 million years old. Granite forms the backbone of the region while other types of Cornish rock, such as serpentine, are found nowhere else in England. The importance of Cornwall's geology is illustrated in its proliferation of Sites of Special Scientific Interest (SSSI) and tangible evidence can be seen at places like Land's End, the Lizard Peninsula and Crackington Haven. Within these rocks can be found the tin and copper that provided the bedrock of Cornwall's economy for many years.

Around 10,000BC Mesolithic hunter-gatherers settled along the coastline around the Lizard and the higher ground of Bodmin. Some 4000 years later there was a marked increase in population with many fortified settlements and monuments built and hedges planted to enclose land for cereal crops.

Cornwall's natural tin and copper reserves began to be utilised in the Bronze Age and artefacts from this period have been excavated at Brea Hill, near Rock, and Gwithian Towans near Hayle.

Iron Age Celts arrived around 600BC and were the dominant race of people for well over 1000 years. Fortified settlements from this period can still be seen at The Rumps and on Trencrom Hill near Carbis Bay.

Perhaps the key moment in the county's history came in 1201 when King John granted the tin miners of Cornwall a charter allowing them special privileges. The miners subsequently wielded considerable power, which emphasised how important tin and copper mining were to the Cornish economy.

At its peak, mining employed about 30 per cent of Cornwall's male workforce, and in the early 19th century the county was the world's greatest producer of copper. In 2006 Cornwall's mining areas gained World Heritage Site status; the remains of mine workings can be seen on several walks in this guidebook – particularly in the Kenidjack Valley near Cape Cornwall.

A number of the beautiful towns and villages strewn across Cornwall (including St Ives, Mousehole, Gorran Haven, Port Isaac and Mullion Cove) were built around harbours, underpinning the value of Cornwall's other key industry – fishing. The 17th, 18th and 19th centuries were a boom time, with millions of fish caught (especially pilchards) and ports flourishing at Falmouth, Fowey, Looe, Padstow, Penzance and St Ives. There are still many working harbours along the coast today, but on a smaller scale.

With mining and fishing now playing a much reduced economic role, tourism has become vital to Cornwall's economy and St Ives, Truro, Falmouth and Newquay remain the most popular destinations for the millions of annual visitors drawn to the region whose people were granted national minority status in 2014.

Wherever you walk the views are enthralling, with buildings such as Godrevy Lighthouse and Truro Cathedral highlighting Cornwall's wonderful heritage. Add to this an astonishing array of flora and fauna – bottlenose and common dolphin, porpoise, gannet, fulmar, cormorant, shag, kittiwake, razorbill, guillemot, puffin, Manx shearwater, chough, teal, greenshank, dunlin, bar-tailed godwit, curlew, oystercatcher, wigeon, heath spotted orchid, birdsfoot trefoil, yellow primroses, pink sea thrift and purple heather and you may well have, in Cornwall, the ultimate walking destination.

How to use this guide

The 40 walks in this guidebook are between 3km and 13km in length and are, therefore, ideal for a morning or evening stroll or an invigorating half-day ramble.

The majority of the routes are coastal, although many run inland and through rolling countryside, woodland and alongside rivers. Much of Cornwall's terrain is hilly, so fitness levels should be taken into consideration before setting out – some of the routes are much tougher than they may appear from the map.

However, Cornwall's network of public paths (including the spectacular South West Coast Path) means navigation is generally simple and the walking good – although any rocky, boggy or steep terrain is detailed in the route descriptions. Because of the path network, a number of the routes are child friendly. It's advisable not to stray from the described routes onto farmland or near cliffs, and where livestock is present dogs must be kept on leads. Many beaches also have seasonal restrictions on access with dogs.

A sketch map for each walk shows the main topographical details of the area and the route. The map is intended to give the reader an idea of the terrain and should not be relied on for navigation – the relevant Ordnance Survey (OS) map should be used for this purpose.

Every route has an estimated round-trip time. This is for rough guidance only and should help in planning, especially when daylight hours are limited. In winter, or after heavy rain, extra time should be added to allow for difficulties underfoot.

Some of the routes in this guidebook are challenging walks, while others cover remote terrain. The weather in Cornwall can change suddenly, while strong winds – particularly along the coast and over higher ground – can occur throughout the year. It's important for all walkers to be aware of the unpredictable nature of the sea while walking on or near Cornwall's cliffs. All of this should be taken into consideration before commencing any of the walks described within this guidebook.

Even in summer, taking some warm, waterproof clothing is advisable and footwear that is comfortable and supportive with good grips is a must. Do not rely on receiving a mobile phone signal when out walking, particularly away from built-up areas.

Wherever possible, the start and finish for each walk is accessible by public transport, and if not there is car parking at or near the start. Most of the car parks mentioned in this guide charge for parking, though it is worth noting that National Trust members can park for free at around 70 National Trust-managed car parks across Cornwall. The majority of the walks are also easily accessed from villages and towns where there are shops, eateries, accommodation and public toilets.

Each route begins with an introduction detailing the terrain, the distance covered, the average time taken to walk the route and the relevant OS map.

Public transport information is also included, although bus routes and timetables can change, so it's best to check before commencing any of the walks in this guide (www.travelinesw.com).

Please also note that although public transport in the area is fairly reliable, it may not run as regularly or as conveniently as necessary for the purposes of these walks. It is especially important to check the running times and departure points of any passenger ferries you intend to use.

South East Cornwall has many coves, inlets and bays, as well as the county's earliest landscaped park.

The River Tamar forms the natural boundary between Cornwall and the rest of the country and at its mouth lies Mount Edgcumbe Country Park. Created by the Earls of Mount Edgcumbe in the 18th century, its managed woodland and parkland sit in sharp contrast to the wild and craggy coastline leading south along the Rame Peninsula, branded as Cornwall's Forgotten Corner. The wide-open spaces and extensive views around Rame Head and Talland Bay, and popular towns and villages such as Polperro and Looe, are characteristic of what walking in Cornwall is all about.

The villages of Fowey and Polruan make great bases for walking. Both locations provided inspiration for the author

Daphne du Maurier, who lived in the area during the early 20th century and wrote her first novel when living near Polruan. Nearby Lantic Bay, Gribbin Head and the River Fowey are all beautiful spots, and the many paths along the coast offer sumptuous views of all three.

Looe was once a thriving port where many of the famous Cornish luggers (fishing vessels) were built. The town is split in two by the River Looe, which provides a focal point to a fascinating walk. Similarly, the coast at Charlestown has many a tale to tell and much of Cornwall's maritime history is detailed at its excellent Shipwreck and Heritage Centre.

As the coast heads south along the Roseland Peninsula it becomes increasingly rugged, particularly when it reaches Gorran Haven and Dodman Point, where the walking is exceptional.

South East Cornwall

Mount Edgcumbe Country Park

Distance 4km **Time** 1 hour 15
Terrain park, woodland paths and tracks
Map OS Explorer 108 **Access** car park at
Cremyll (parking charge); regular foot
passenger ferry from Admirals Hard in
Plymouth to Cremyll; bus (34) from Royal
Parade (city centre) to Admirals Hard;
cruises also operate from Plymouth's
historic Barbican area to Cremyll

Mount Edgcumbe lies just inside Cornwall
on the northeastern fringes of the Rame
Peninsula overlooking Plymouth Sound.
Paths criss-cross the park and woodland,
passing numerous listed structures,
formal gardens, a deer park, an 18th-
century folly and, at the park's centre, the
striking Mount Edgcumbe House.

The walk begins at the village of Cremyll
by the River Tamar, accessed by a short
breezy boat ride from Plymouth. A ferry
service linking Cornwall and Devon has
been in existence here since medieval
times, although Mount Edgcumbe was,
until 1854, part of Devon.

From the quay, enter Mount Edgcumbe
Country Park through the large entrance
gate. Follow The Avenue to a junction, go
straight on and climb to a fork. A left turn
takes you to Mount Edgcumbe House
(open daily April-September, except
Fridays and Saturdays).

Built within the existing deer park
between 1547 and 1553 for Sir Richard
Edgcumbe of Cotehele, the house is
beautifully furnished with famous
paintings, 16th-century tapestries and
Bronze Age artefacts. The Victorian East
Lawn Terrace gives magnificent views over
the Sound.

Return to the main drive and continue,
going straight on at a crossroads and then
right at a next fork. After a car park, bear
left onto a woodland track (signposted
Deer Park) which climbs uphill, passing
through a gate onto a grassy track. Follow
this across farmland (where livestock graze)

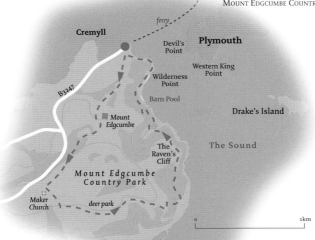

and through a gate just before the 12th-century Maker Church. Turn left and, where the path splits after another gate, turn left again to continue over farmland, keeping right at the next fork. Fallow deer can be spotted here, having roamed freely since 1515 when Henry VIII granted Sir Piers Edgcumbe permission to empark them.

At the next two forks, keep right and then pass through a gate into woodland. Go down steps and turn left past an old stone building north of Picklecombe Point. Follow a well-maintained path downhill and through a gate to pick up the Zig-Zags, where you walk down some steps, before swinging sharp left.

Keep left at the next fork to gain a rough road beside the impressive Lady Emma's Cottage, which was built in 1882. During Victorian times this was a tearoom.

Follow the road past the folly perched on a steep slope to the left – it was built as a picturesque ruin in 1747 from which to enjoy the expansive view along the Tamar. Once through a gate, fork right into woodland and, at a junction, take a right turn. Walk down a road past a pond and the Ionic Temple of Milton, which contains an inscription from John Milton's epic poem *Paradise Lost*.

Turn left to follow another park road along the coast, passing the magnificent gardens, bounded by high hedges and laid out between 1750 and 1809 by the Earls of Mount Edgcumbe in Italian, English and French styles. Once past The Orangery – built in the mid-18th century to house orange trees from Constantinople, and now a restaurant – continue out of the park and back to Cremyll.

◀ Mount Edgcumbe Folly

Cawsand to Rame Head

Distance 8.75km **Time** 2 hours 30 **Terrain** minor roads, coastal and countryside paths **Map** OS Explorer 108 **Access** car park at Cawsand (parking charge); buses from Torpoint, Cremyll and Plymouth to Cawsand; a seasonal foot passenger ferry also runs from Plymouth Barbican to Cawsand Beach (subject to weather)

The Rame Peninsula is sometimes known as 'Cornwall's Forgotten Corner' as it sits off the well-trodden path at the county's southeastern edge. This peaceful walk follows cliff paths and country roads to reach an atmospheric headland chapel almost entirely surrounded by sea.

The adjoining seaside villages of Cawsand and Kingsand are practically one, though until 1844 only Cawsand was in Cornwall as Kingsand was over the border in Devon. Their narrow streets sloping down to two small but busy bays are well

worth exploring. Cawsand Fort dominates the villages, built in the 1860s as part of Lord Palmerston's Royal Commission on the Defence of the United Kingdom as a result of concerns that the French were preparing to invade. When it became clear that France had no such intention, this and other defences became collectively known as Palmerston's Follies. Cawsand Fort is now residential accommodation.

From Cawsand car park, exit left onto St Andrews Place and walk downhill through the village. Once past St Andrews Church turn right onto Pier Lane, which rises gradually past several houses, giving views over Plymouth Sound, before becoming a path as it passes into woodland.

The path then joins a narrow road. Follow this and, after Bayfield Cottage, bear right onto a stony track, going left onto another narrow road at the next junction. This takes you past the entrance of an old signal house, then onto cliffs above Penlee

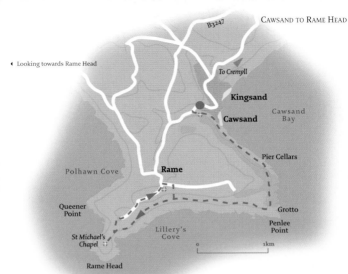

◄ Looking towards Rame Head

B3247

To Cremyll

Kingsand

Cawsand Bay

Cawsand

Pier Cellars

Polhawn Cove

Rame

Queener Point

Grotto

Penlee Point

St Michael's Chapel ✝

Lillery's Cove

0   1km

Rame Head

Point – with spectacular views towards Rame Head. A track leads west, passing through a pocket of woodland. When it swings right, go straight on through a gate onto a path, which undulates easily along the clifftop. After around 2km, it drops gently down past a radio mast and a couple of benches. A final steep pull up steps leads onto Rame Head with its beautifully preserved chapel.

Dedicated to the archangel St Michael, it is thought that the chapel dates from medieval times, although Mass took place here as far back as 1397. There is evidence that this area has been occupied for far longer – flints found around here have been dated to the Mesolithic period. With views across Whitsand Bay towards Looe and sea all around, this is a lonely,

windswept and atmospheric vantage point.

Retrace your steps down to the benches, keep left onto a grassy path and climb steadily to Rame Head National Coastwatch building. Go through a gate and past a car park onto a minor road which is followed to the lovely Rame Church. Dedicated to St Germanus, the German bishop who supposedly landed at Rame around 400AD, the first stone church was consecrated in 1259. The present-day building has no electricity and is lit by candles.

Once past the church, turn right onto the side road (which eventually leads to the former Battery, now a nature reserve, at Penlee Point); after 30m leave this road for a field-edge path on the right, descending through a gate to the outward path. Turn left and retrace your steps to Cawsand.

11

Around Looe

Distance 5km **Time** 1 hour 30
Terrain pavement and paths; steep sections
Map OS Explorer 107 **Access** several car
parks in Looe (parking charges); regular
buses and trains from Liskeard to Looe

**Separated by its busy river, East and West
Looe combine to form the fishing town of
Looe which in Victorian times became a
popular tourist destination and remains so
to this day. Looe is full of character and this
walk explores its compact, lively streets.**

Both East and West Looe had separate
parliamentary seats during the 12th
century, and it wasn't until 1411 that a
wooden bridge connected both banks of
the river. When this burned down, it was
replaced by a 14-arch stone bridge. The
current seven-arch bridge was opened in
1853, by which time Looe had become a
thriving port, exporting tin and granite,

and home to fishing and shipbuilding
industries. Many of the famous Cornish
'luggers' were built here during the 19th
and early 20th centuries; these were open
boats with two or three sails and they were
hand-crafted, meaning no two boats were
the same.

From Looe Railway Station, turn left,
then make a right turn into the district of
Shutta, thought to have been Looe's
original settlement. Turn right again onto
the narrow Shutta Road, which climbs
steeply past several distinctive houses
until high above East Looe.

The incline eases on approach to a
junction, where you go straight down
Shutta Road as it drops towards the town
centre. At an old well, as the road sweeps
right, bear left onto a paved path. Climb
steps and continue to Barbican Hill
(thought to be from the Latin *Barbecana*,

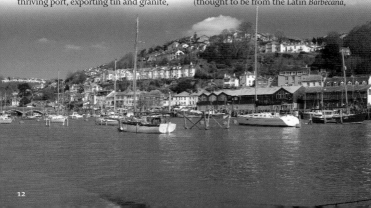

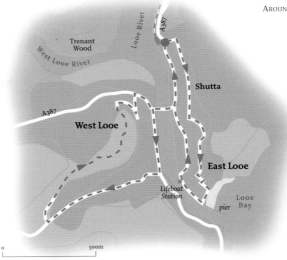

meaning 'the outer fortification of a city or castle').

Turn right to descend steeply down Castle Street and then Tower Hill to Higher Market Street where you turn left to reach a car park at East Looe Beach. Keep right to reach the RNLI station at the end and right again here to follow the quayside on Buller Street which veers away from the water to then curve onto Fore Street. Make your way along this tight, busy street to reach the old stone bridge at the corner of Station Road.

This takes you across the river into West Looe, where you go left onto Quay Road to head back downstream with good views over the houses of East Looe built steeply into the hillside. Just before Hannafore Road, turn right onto West

Looe Hill and make the steep climb up narrow streets.

After turning right onto Downs Lane, the gradient eases and a panoramic view along the River Looe is the reward for your efforts. The road soon narrows to a lane and this continues high above the town. After passing through a gate, a path takes you onwards through woods and crosses an area of grassland and a small car park.

Go down steps here, then make two left turns onto a narrow road. After a short distance, bear right and walk down Farmer's Hill, dropping steeply to West Road, where you turn right. At North Road take a left and then right onto Polperro Road, which is followed back into East Looe, crossing the river to Station Road and returning to the railway station.

Smugglers' coast from Polperro

**Distance 6.5km Time 2 hours
Terrain** minor roads, countryside and coast
paths; steep steps **Map** OS Explorer 107
Access car park at Crumplehorn (parking
charge); regular buses from Liskeard and
Looe to Polperro

**A superb walk that uses the South West
Coast Path and quiet roads to link
Polperro with Talland Bay.**

The village of Polperro is built around a
natural inlet, bound on three sides by
steep hillside. This landscape made
Polperro a haven for smugglers during the
18th century, when duty on goods was
deemed excessive. Local fishermen began
importing and exporting goods such as
tea, gin, brandy and tobacco from
Guernsey; smuggling became a thriving
business, much of it organised by

Zephaniah Job – a local merchant who
became known as the 'smuggler's banker'
due to the prosperity he brought to the
village. Ships were loaded and unloaded in
all weathers, usually at night without
lights at Talland Bay.

From the large car park at Crumplehorn,
exit right to take the A387 to a roundabout,
where you go straight onto The Coombe to
follow the pavement past Polperro Village
Hall into the snug confines of the village.

Carry on along Fore Street, turning right
onto Big Green opposite the post office.
Take a left onto Lansallos Street to reach
Polperro's lovely harbour – a popular spot
for artists. Turn left, then right onto The
Warren and make your way alongside the
harbour, passing the excellent Polperro
Heritage Museum of Smuggling and
Fishing, which details the village's history

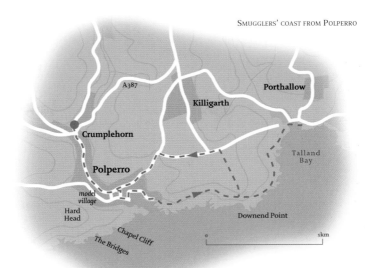

through exhibits and photographs (open Easter until October).

The Warren climbs steeply out of Polperro to a path on the right, known as Reuben's Walk. Follow this along the craggy coast to a fork where you can detour right to a distinctive lighthouse. Continuing on Reuben's Walk, you come to several flights of steep steps which you climb to gain the South West Coast Path.

Turn right here towards Talland Bay and, where the path splits, go right again, signposted for Talland (left is for Killigarth). A well-maintained path, lined with bluebells, thrift and primrose in spring and summer, passes a war memorial and continues northeast to a junction. Turn right, walk along a road and, once around a barrier, go right down a

steep path to reach lovely Talland Bay, where there's a beach café.

Retrace your steps to the Talland/ Killigarth junction. Turn right for Killigarth and climb a steep path above Downend Point. At another sign for Killigarth, go left up steps and follow a path between a fence and a wall. Bear right over a stile, then walk left along a field-edge path (where livestock may be grazing).

Beyond a gate, turn left onto a single-track road beside a caravan park. At a junction go straight on along the pavement to pass Polperro Primary School and onto Brentwartha, where the road narrows. Drop steeply to a junction and turn left onto Talland Hill, where another steep descent leads back into Polperro at Fore Street. Retrace your steps to the start.

Creeks and coves of Polruan

Distance 7km **Time** 2 hours 15
Terrain minor roads, coastal and
woodland paths **Map** OS Explorer 107
Access several car parks in Fowey (parking
charges); bus from Looe to Polruan and
seasonal ferry (April to October) from
Mevagissey to Fowey; ferry services from
Fowey to Polruan

This walk explores the diverse landscape
that inspired Daphne du Maurier to write
many of her classic novels. The steep
slopes and coastal path around Polruan
give great views along the way.

Polruan's history of fishing and
boatbuilding dates back many centuries –
there is still a working boatyard beside the
harbour – but it is perhaps best known for
its proximity to a residence of the author

Daphne du Maurier. The du Mauriers
moved to Bodinnick in 1927 when she wrote
her first book, *The Loving Spirit*, published in
1931. They moved to Fowey in 1943.

Polruan can be reached by road, but
the best approach is by ferry from Fowey
Quay. From the harbour, follow The Quay
to East Street, turn left and then go right
onto Hall Walk.

After climbing several flights of steps,
walk right up a narrow street as it climbs
steeply onto a path. At the top of the climb
turn left and continue to Meadow Close,
where you get a good view of Polruan and
Fowey. Make another left and drop left
again down steps where the street ends,
then take a right onto a woodland path.

Follow this through the National Trust
land of North Downs. At a T-junction, turn

16

◀ Fowey from Polruan

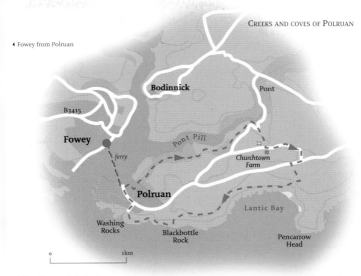

Bodinnick

Pont

B3415

Fowey

ferry

Pont Pill

Churchtown
Farm

Polruan

Lantic Bay

Washing
Rocks

Blackbottle
Rock

Pencarrow
Head

0   1km

right, then go left for Pont and Bodinnick.
Keep left at the next fork for fine views
over the River Fowey. Once down several
flights of steps, climb to a minor road a
little south of Pont.

Turn left and then go right through a
gate beside Little Churchtown Farm.
A sustained ascent takes you up to a
gate into the grounds of the Church of
St Wyllow, named after a Christian hermit
who lived in Pont around 596AD. It is said
that St Wyllow was killed by a relative who
then decided to build a church in his
honour. The present-day building dates
from the 14th century and the main tower
stands over 20m tall.

Turn left from the churchyard, follow a
minor road downhill and then steeply back
up through pleasant countryside to
eventually reach a junction just

after Pencarrow car park. Cross the road,
go through a gate, along a roadside path
to the right and through another gate
before turning left along a field-edge path.
Follow this and turn right just before
a third gate.

From here a path runs west, high
above Lantic Bay. After a short descent,
a long, gradual climb takes you through
several gates before you get to the
highest point with its views over Lantic Bay
and Gribbin Head.

The well-maintained path drops down
through several more gates, eventually
crossing a field to reach the outskirts of
Polruan. Exit right through a gate, then go
straight on and down School Lane to
Speakers Corner. Turn right (still on School
Lane), then left onto Fore Street to return
to Polruan Harbour.

Fowey and Gribbin Head

Distance 11.75km **Time** 3 hours 30
Terrain minor roads, countryside and
coastal paths; steps **Map** OS Explorer 107
Access several car parks in Fowey (parking
charges); regular bus from St Austell to
Fowey; daily ferry service from Polruan to
Fowey and summer ferry service from
Mevagissey to Fowey

**Fowey (pronounced 'foy') is a picturesque
town on the banks of the River Fowey
situated within an Area of Outstanding
Natural Beauty. Part of the return uses the
43km-long Saints Way, where ancient paths
connect standing stones, Neolithic
hillforts, holy wells and churches.**

From the 13th century Fowey was
Cornwall's principal port, exporting tin,
wool and fish. Its proud military history
also extends back to this time, when
Fowey provided more large ships for Royal
Service than London. Occupations such as
shipbuilding, rope and sailcloth making

were vital in the town's early development.

From Fowey Quay follow Market
Street left onto Lostwithiel Street, then
go left again onto Esplanade. Continue
for around 750m to Readymoney Cove.
Climb up a lane past St Catherine's
Cottage, then go left at a junction into
Covington Woods.

Climb a rocky path, branching left at a
fork for Gribbin Head. Pass the ruin of
St Catherine's Castle (built by Henry VIII
in 1536 as an artillery fort), with views to
Polruan. Bear right at a fork, then take the
path in the middle at a three-way junction.
At the next junction, go left through a gate
onto a field-edge path and follow this
southwest towards Gribbin Head.

Continuing around Coombe Haven, pass
through a few gates and cross two stiles to
reach Southground Point. After another
stile, the path leads you down steps to
sandy Polridmouth Cove. Go left at a
junction, cross stepping stones over the

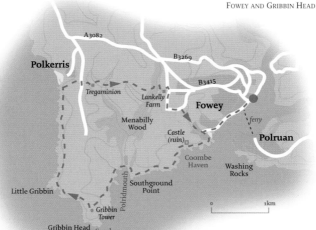

outflow from the private ornamental lake and take a left at another junction. The path eventually climbs steeply onto Gribbin Head (from the Cornish for 'Little Ridge') with its 26m-high red-and-white navigational tower and extensive views across St Austell Bay.

After the tower, a gate gives access to a stunning high-level cliff walk heading northwest, then north above St Austell Bay. The path hugs the cliffs, passing through several gates as it descends gently before rising steadily towards Polkerris. Now heading inland above the village, go through a gate to carry straight on along a field path, keeping right of woodland. (If in need of refreshment, detour down the Coast Path to the pretty harbour beach at Polkerris, where there's a pub and café.)

After another gate, turn right onto a minor road and then left onto the Saints Way.

Follow the road, shortly turning right at Tregaminion – be considerate as this is a working farm. After passing through a gate, go left through two more gates. A path leads you down over a footbridge, beyond which you continue along the right edge of a field, climbing steep steps to Trenant Cottage. The route continues through pleasant countryside, before descending through woodland. Go under an old railway arch and past Lankelly Farm before turning right at a minor road.

After passing the entrance to Fowey Rugby Club, turn left onto a narrow road. Just before a house turn right onto Love Lane, which descends through Covington Woods. Carry straight on at a junction to reach your outward path above Readymoney Cove. Turn left, passing the sheltered, sandy beach to return to Fowey.

◀ Polruan from near Fowey

Charlestown to Porthpean

Distance 4.25km **Time** 1 hour 30
Terrain minor roads, countryside and
coastal paths; some steep sections
Map OS Explorer 107 **Access** Shipwreck and
Heritage Centre car park (parking charge);
regular bus from St Austell to Charlestown

Quiet roads and paths link the villages
of Charlestown and Porthpean. This
walk begins from the excellent Shipwreck
and Heritage Centre, which details
Charlestown's fascinating maritime
history, the industries that have been
crucial to its survival and the many ships
that have met their end along the Cornish
coast. The museum is open daily from
March to November. The neighbouring
villages of Higher and Lower Porthpean
are a peaceful contrast to this lively port.

Charlestown was once known as West
Polmear, but between 1790 and 1810 local
landowner Charles Rashleigh developed it
(and subsequently named it after himself),
primarily for the export of copper and
china clay. The 19th century saw the village
become a remarkably busy port, with
boatbuilding, ropemaking, brickworks,
lime burning and pilchard curing just
some of the harbourside industries.

From the museum car park, turn right
onto Charlestown Road, then left onto
Duporth Road. After a few cottages, keep
right at a junction to continue along
Duporth Road on a steep climb through
woodland, with roadside verges soon
giving way to pavement. After 750m, turn
left onto Porthpean Road.

Beyond St Austell Community Hospital,

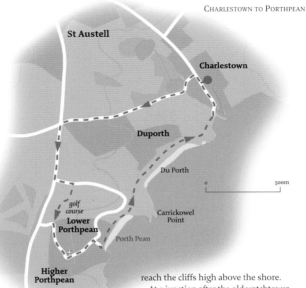

turn left onto Porthpean Beach Road, looking for a public bridleway for Higher Porthpean on the right in around 200m. This runs to the right of a golf course to meet a narrow road, where you go left to drop down into the village, sweeping left past the lovely St Leven's Church with its distinctive steeple and gate.

The road now descends quite steeply, bound on both sides by hedges, to a road on the right opposite a car park. Take this to reach the coast at Porthpean Sailing Club and go left onto a coastal path. Follow the sea wall above Porthpean Beach, turning left up steep steps to reach the cliffs high above the shore.

At a junction after the old watchtower, turn left with fine views of the houses of Lower Porthpean stacked on the hillside above the ragged coastline. Once over a footbridge continue along the clifftop, passing several houses. Beyond a gate, the path sweeps left to Crinnis Head, home to Charlestown Gun Battery, which was built in 1793 after Charles Rashleigh decided it was required to defend the harbour. It was also used as a lookout for shoals of pilchards.

Turn right through a gate to walk through the battery, bearing left to reach a gap in the wall. A flight of steps descends steeply, with good views over Charlestown Harbour, which you reach via a gate. Follow Charlestown Road back to the museum.

◀ Charlestown Harbour

Gorran Haven and Dodman Point

Distance 6.5km **Time** 2 hours
Terrain minor roads, coastal and
countryside paths **Map** OS Explorer 107
Access car park at Gorran Haven (parking
charge) (also National Trust car park at
Lamledra); limited bus service from
St Austell to Gorran Haven

**Cornwall's coastline features many coves,
bays, inlets and some lovely secluded
villages. One of the most attractive of
these is Gorran Haven, which sits beneath
the cliffs on the eastern edge of the
Roseland Peninsula. At the peninsula's
southern tip is Dodman Point, the highest
headland on the south Cornish coast,
with some far-reaching views.**

Turn left from the car park and walk
down Canton towards the harbour at
Gorran Haven. The village used to be called
Portheast – a corruption of Port Just – and
was possibly named after an early
Christian saint. Portheast was recorded in

the 13th century for catching pilchards in
long nets, a process known as 'seining'.
When, in the late 18th century, Portheast
became known as Gorran Haven it was
already an important centre for fishing.

Just before the harbour take a right onto
Foxhole Lane, then go straight up steps,
turning left at a sign for Lamledra. A path
takes you away from the village and, once
through a gate, a field-edge path continues
along cliffs with views over Gorran Haven.

After another gate, continue around the
rocky headland of Pen-a-maen. Branch
right at a fork to climb up and pass
through a gate, continuing over open
hillside above the long sandy finger of
Vault Beach. A gradual ascent leads to
another fork where you go left to follow
the path past a wall, then through three
gates into Dodman, which is cared for by
the National Trust.

Continue south, where you may spot
Shetland and Dartmoor ponies and, after

◄ Gorran Haven

passing through two gates, sweep right to a fork and marker post. Go left to gain the summit of Dodman Point with its large granite cross, erected in 1896 by Rev G Martin as a navigational aid for seafarers. Dodman Point is also home to a huge Iron Age earthwork, thought to have housed a large cliff castle some 2000 years ago.

Retrace your steps to the marker post and turn left, bearing northwest above Lizard Pool to a gate on the right, signposted for Penare. Go inland here on a grassy, and at times boggy, track known as The Bulwark, which is enclosed on either side by steep embankments. In a while, the path veers left through a gate onto a rougher track, which drops down through another gate to Penare.

Turning right, a narrow road takes you through the hamlet to a junction. Go straight on through a gate for Treveague, following a fenced path through two gates, then past Treveague farm and campsite. Make a right at a junction, then left onto a track for Gorran Haven. The path passes through a gate and drops down through scrubby woodland, before going through another gate and over a burn. After a final gate, turn right and then left onto a road. A right turn onto Rice Lane takes you back into Gorran Haven.

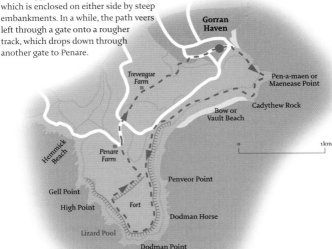

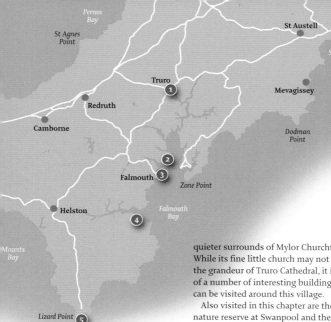

Perran
Bay

St Agnes
Point

St Austell

Fowe

St Austell
Bay

Gribb
Poin

Truro

Mevagissey

Redruth

Camborne

Dodman
Point

Falmouth

Zone Point

Helston

Falmouth
Bay

Mounts
Bay

Lizard Point

The historic city of Truro is dominated by its eye-catching cathedral with a central spire climbing to 75m in height. Much of South Cornwall's public transport infrastructure passes through the county capital (and Cornwall's s only city), making it an ideal base for enjoying a number of great walks that extend along the coast and to mainland Britain's southernmost point.

Woodland and riverbank paths lead around Truro's southern edge, offering great wildlife-watching opportunities. Similar paths circumnavigate the much

quieter surrounds of Mylor Churchtown. While its fine little church may not have the grandeur of Truro Cathedral, it is one of a number of interesting buildings that can be visited around this village.

Also visited in this chapter are the small nature reserve at Swanpool and the clifftops that drop down into Maenporth, while woodland again dominates the coastline between the village of Helford and the secluded hamlet of St Anthony-in-Meneage, beside Gillan Creek.

However, for wildlife (as well as some of the finest scenery in Cornwall), Lizard Point, Cornwall's southern tip, and Kynance Cove are hard to match – seals, Manx shearwaters, shag, fulmar and the Cornish chough are just a few examples of what you might see. The chough, with its distinctive red legs and bill, has had a close association with the Duchy of Cornwall for several hundred years and it features on the Cornish Coat of Arms.

Truro and the south

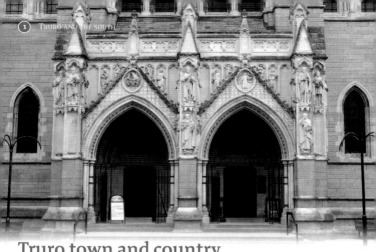

Truro town and country

Distance 6.5km **Time** 2 hours
Terrain pavement, countryside and
riverbank paths **Map** OS Explorer 105
Access car parking in Truro (charges);
Truro is well served by public transport

The city of Truro is Cornwall's main
administrative centre and a lovely place
to wander around. It has a rich history
and some fine buildings – not least the
magnificent Truro Cathedral, which
dominates the immediate landscape. To
the south and west, quiet countryside
and riverbank paths provide a nice
contrast to the busy city streets.

Begin from the entrance of Truro
Cathedral, which was completed in 1910,
some 30 years after the Duke of Cornwall
(later Edward VII) laid the foundation
stone. It was the first cathedral to be built
on a new site since Salisbury was built in

1220 and its central spire climbs to a
height of 75m. Truro itself dates back to
around the 12th century when Richard
Luci, Chief Justice of England, built a
castle here. By the 1300s Truro was one of
Cornwall's five stannary towns and was,
therefore, entrusted with collecting tin
coinage for the Duchy of Cornwall or
the Crown.

From the 17th century the Truro River
made Truro prosperous, with industries
such as tin smelting, pottery and carpet
making, and from the 18th century
Truro was part of Cornwall's thriving tin
mining industry.

Turn left onto High Cross, then right
onto Cathedral Lane. Cross St Nicholas
Street to follow Lemon Street, then take a
left onto Lemon Quay. Walk along here
and, after passing under the A39, go left
and then right onto Riverside Walk,

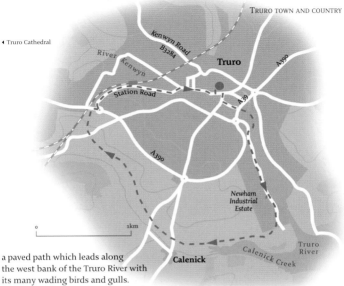

◀ Truro Cathedral

Truro

Kenwyn Road

B3284

A390

River Kenwyn

Station Road

A39

A390

Newham Industrial Estate

Calenick

Calenick Creek

Truro River

0   1km

a paved path which leads along the west bank of the Truro River with its many wading birds and gulls.

The path continues between the river and houses, before swinging right to Newham Road. Turn left to follow the pavement for around 250m, then go right onto Gas Hill and after just a few metres bear left onto National Cycle Network Route 3. Once through a gate, pick up a wooded path, which follows the course of the old Newham Railway Line.

In a while, cross a road where the path (signposted 'Redruth') continues south and then west through lovely wildlife-rich countryside. After 1.75km, go through two gates on either side of a single-track road just north of Calenick, and shortly afterwards cross a bridge over the A39.

After another 1km, the path crosses a bridge over a minor road and then swings right through a gate. Turn left onto a track, which soon veers right onto a path. This climbs gently past County Hall (the headquarters of Cornwall Council) and through a gate onto Highertown.

Turn right, then cross Highertown beside a roundabout to join Station Road, which descends towards the city centre past the impressive Old County Hall (the previous headquarters of Cornwall Council and now a Grade II listed building) and Truro Railway Station, onto Richmond Hill. At a mini-roundabout, go straight on and continue onto River Street, then go left onto St Nicholas Street, where a left turn onto King Street leads back to the cathedral.

27

Mylor and the Carrick Roads

Distance 6.5km **Time** 2 hours
Terrain minor roads, woodland and
countryside paths **Map** OS Explorer 105
Access car park at Mylor Churchtown
(parking charge); regular buses from
Falmouth to Mylor Churchtown

A mostly gentle walk from the village of
Mylor Churchtown. Coastal paths lead
along the Carrick Roads, the outer tidal
basin of the Fal Estuary – one of the world's
largest natural harbours – to Flushing and
the Penryn River, where quiet paths and
roads continue to Trelew and Mylor Creek.

Exit left from Mylor Yacht Club car park
and walk through the village, passing
Mylor Church and the harbour. The
church was founded in 411AD and
dedicated to St Melorus, with the present
building dating from the late 19th
century. Today the harbour is home to
400 berths, but was originally the most
westerly naval dockyard in England, as

well as an operations base for the French
Resistance during the Second World War.

The road shortly narrows onto a public
footpath for Flushing. At a three-way
junction, go left past Restronguet Sailing
Club and, once over a stile, continue along
a field-edge path through Trefusis Estate
alongside the Carrick Roads – a deep
channel that is navigable all the way from
Falmouth to Truro.

After a stile, the path rounds Penarrow
Point, then heads south for 1.5km, with
views across the water to St Anthony
Head at the tip of the Roseland Peninsula.
Beyond another stile, go round Trefusis
Point, looking across to Falmouth's docks.
Head west into Kilnquay Wood, crossing a
granite stile onto a track. At a narrow road
make a left, walk past Flushing & Mylor
Pilot Gig Club, then go through a gate to
reach the small village of Flushing at
Trefusis Road, following this past some
distinctive houses.

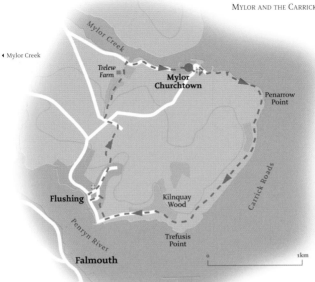

◀ Mylor Creek

As the road begins to descend, fork right onto a track for Flushing Bowling Club, leading uphill through a gate and then an area of parkland. After another gate, steps lead down to a road. Turn left at the bottom and left again at a junction to return to Trefusis Road – this takes you through Flushing village centre, past colourful houses and a small harbour.

Turn right onto Kersey Road, which soon rises steeply to Orchard Vale. Bear left up steps onto a narrow path signed for Mylor Church and cross a stile onto a path which follows the left edge of a field all the way to another stile by a house.

Go over the stile and through a gate on your right, turning left beside a cattle grid to follow the road to a crossroads. Go straight on here and, after 20m, turn right over a stile onto a footpath for Trelew. This descends into woodland; at a fork keep right, drop downhill and pass through a gate, then keep straight on to a junction. Go left, climb steps onto a broader track, then turn right. Beyond a gate, turn right onto a narrow road and walk past the scattering of houses at Trelew, alongside Mylor Creek and back to Mylor Churchtown. At a junction, go straight across into the grounds of Mylor Church and follow the path through the churchyard to exit at a gate. Turn left to return to the start.

Swanpool to Maenporth

Distance 6.25km **Time** 1 hour 30
Terrain minor road, pavement, coastal
paths **Map** OS Explorer 103 **Access** bus
from Falmouth to Swanpool Beach; car
park at Swanpool (parking charge)

Begin at Swanpool on the outskirts of
Falmouth to loop around a small nature
reserve – a Site of Special Scientific
Interest – before following the clifftops to
the peaceful cove of Maenporth and its
secluded sandy beach.

The centrepiece of Swanpool Nature
Reserve dates back to the last ice age,
when a shingle bar separated a freshwater
lagoon from the sea. It was three times
larger than and three times the depth of
the pool seen here today, but in 1826 a
culvert was dug through the shingle bar,
draining much of the water into the sea.
At high spring tides seawater rises above
the culvert and flows into Swanpool,
creating the mix of fresh and salt water
that makes this such a perfect habitat for
a range of wildlife; there have been more
than 100 bird species recorded here.

On the water you might spot coot,
moorhen, mallard, tufted ducks, swan and
little grebe, whilst the surrounding
woodland and reedbeds play host to
water rail, siskin, kingfisher and small
tortoiseshell butterfly. The wetter fringes
of the reserve are ideal for yellow flag iris,
Cornish moneywort, greater tussock
sedge and cuckoo flower to grow.

From the car park across the road from

Swanpool Beach, face the white ticket office and turn left to cross the car park with the lagoon on your right. Turn right onto a quiet road and, when you reach the head of the pool, bear right onto a pavement for views across the water, reedbeds and woodland. Follow the pavement south along the pool's east bank to the car park.

Carry on along Swanpool Road, passing the sandy cove and public toilets. Climb steeply past a couple of houses, then turn left onto the waymarked path for Maenporth. This fenced path climbs gradually alongside fields, bearing right at two forks, with views of Swanpool, Falmouth and St Anthony Head opening out. Continue into a pleasant pocket of woodland above Pennance Point, where you branch right to reach a junction. Go right again and follow a well-made path southwest through hedgerows and gorse, high above the coast.

Above Newport Head, the outlook extends down into Maenporth and south towards the peninsula of Rosemullion Head. A gradual and then steeper descent takes you through a gate to arrive at Maenporth. Turn left to reach the lovely sandy beach and a café.

Surrounding the cove are weathered, sea-battered cliffs, which contain several caves. At low tides the wreck of *Ben Asdale*, which sank off Maenporth in 1978, can be seen and even walked out to. To return to Swanpool simply retrace your steps along the South West Coast Path.

◀ Swanpool and Falmouth

Helford and St Anthony-in-Meneage

Distance 8km **Time** 2 hours 30
Terrain minor roads, woodland and coast
paths **Map** OS Explorer 103 **Access** limited
bus service from Helston to Helford; a
seasonal passenger ferry (April to October)
operates between Helford and Helford
Passage, as well as pre-booked water
taxis further afield; car park at Helford
(parking charge)

**This tough walk meanders from the
idyllic village of Helford along woodland
and coastal paths to the parish of St
Anthony-in-Meneage on the banks of
Gillan Creek.**

Sited on the south bank of the Helford
River, at the northern edge of the Lizard
Peninsula, Helford retains a quiet, unspoilt
beauty. Only authorised vehicles can enter
the village, and the many thatched cottages
add to its charm. The Helford River is a
Marine Conservation Area, which means the

diverse marine life along this beautiful
stretch of water is protected. The pedestrian
ferry service that runs between Helford and
Helford Passage has been in existence since
the Middle Ages.

From the car park entrance, cross a narrow
road, then turn left through a gate onto a
woodland path. This leads you past Helford
River Sailing Club, through a gate and, after
a while, down some steps onto a minor
road. Turn right and climb steadily through
woodland, leaving the road when it sweeps
right for a rough path (on the left) bearing
east by the Helford River.

Taking the right branch at a fork, climb
steeply through woodland before heading
back down steps to the riverbank. After
rounding the secluded coves of Ponsence
and Bosahan (which lies at the foot of the
sub-tropical Bosahan Garden and is open
in summer, accessed from Manaccan), the
woods are eventually left behind as the

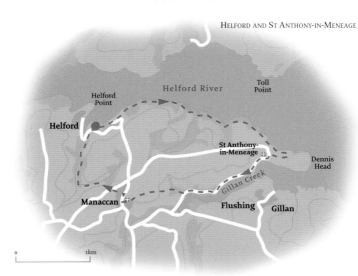

path climbs through a gate into a field.

Once across two stiles and two more fields, a short, steep pull through scrubby woodland brings you to another gate. Go through this and the next gate, before turning right just before Dennis Head to go down the left edge of a field. Enjoy the view of Gillan Creek before bearing right onto a track and dropping down through a gate into St Anthony-in-Meneage.

Cross the road and follow a path onto another narrow road, which leads through the hamlet and past the 12th-century St Anthony's Church, reputedly built by appreciative Normans who found safety in Gillan Creek after a fierce storm.

The road heads southwest through the woods above Gillan Creek, bearing left after around 1.25km – here, take a sharp right through a gate onto a wooded public path.

After a while, it becomes a rough lane and then the narrow Vicarage Lane, continuing to the small village of Manaccan. At a T-junction go straight on through a gate into the grounds of the church, famous for the thriving fig tree growing out of part of the wall. Exit through another gate, go straight on, then turn right at a junction. Climb a narrow road past Manaccan Primary School and at Minster Meadow turn left. Continue onto a path which runs along the right edge of a field.

Cross a stile onto a road and turn left, then right over a stile. The path crosses a field, skirting woodland to the right, and over three stiles. At a fork go right onto a muddy track which eventually returns to Helford. Carry straight on along a road as it rises steeply back to the car park.

◀ Gillan Creek, St Anthony-in-Meneage

Kynance Cove and Lizard Point

Distance 9km **Time** 3 hours **Terrain** cliff
paths and tracks **Map** OS Explorer 103
Access bus from Helston to Lizard; free car
park at Lizard (but donations welcome)

This walk, which visits the National
Trust-owned Kynance Cove and Lizard
Point, the southernmost tip of the British
mainland, is arguably the finest in
Cornwall. Great paths, exceptional views,
unique geology, abundant wildlife and a
visit to Lloyds Signal Station make it an
absolute gem.

The walk begins from the village of
Lizard, a remote outpost with a laid-back
air. From the car park follow Pentreath
Lane past public toilets and several
houses. At a signpost for Kynance Cove
bear right, climb some steps onto a raised
path and follow this across a field. After
going back down some steps, head right

where the path splits and climb gradually
between hedgerows and over two stiles.
A broad grassy path crosses a field and
another stile onto a single-track road. Go
straight on past a house and then bear
right where a path crosses open country.

At a track go straight across into Kynance
Cove car park, turn right at a flagpole and
descend a fairly steep path to Kynance
Cove – surely Cornwall's most picturesque
beach, though it can be submerged at high
tide and care must be taken if exploring its
caves and arches, especially around
Asparagus Island, which is only accessible
on a falling tide with very high cliffs to the
west. Over to the north are the Devil's
Letterbox and the Bellows, which are
impressive if the tide is right. The lovely
café in the cove is open in summer.

Retrace your steps until you reach a
path for Lizard Point, then turn right and

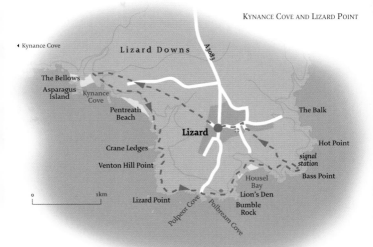

◄ Kynance Cove

Lizard Downs

A 3083

The Bellows

Asparagus Island

Kynance Cove

Pentreath Beach

The Balk

Lizard

Crane Ledges

Venton Hill Point

Hot Point

signal station

Bass Point

Housel Bay

Lion's Den

Bumble Rock

Lizard Point

Polpeor Cove

Polbream Cove

0   1km

climb steep steps for stunning views along the coast. From here, a path hugs the cliffs, awash with colourful sea campion, sea pinks and kidney vetch during spring and summer. The geology here includes serpentine rock, which is found nowhere else in England, and Old Lizard Head mica schist, which is around 500 million years old.

Continue southeast and then south for almost 2km, crossing three stiles, for views of Lizard Point on rounding Old Lizard Head. The path drops down past Polpeor Cove – a good point to spot seals, Manx shearwater, shag, fulmar and chough, which, after an absence of more than 30 years, returned to breed in 2002. The chough, a member of the crow family, is a particularly important bird in Cornwall – it is said to hold the spirit of King Arthur.

Once over a footbridge, go up steps onto

a path to pass a café, car park and Lizard Lighthouse (though this wasn't built until 1751, a light has been guiding boats along this treacherous coastline since 1619). As the path rounds the headland above Bumble Rock, the path runs close to the collapsed sea cave of Lion's Den, where care should be taken. A steep descent to the crystal-clear waters of Housel Bay follows.

After crossing another footbridge, turn left up steps, then right at a junction where the path continues towards Lloyds Signal Station. Once through a gate, turn right onto the rough track of Lloyds Road, which leads to the oldest surviving operational wireless station in the world. It was here in 1901 that Guglielmo Marconi started his experiments to send wireless signals across the Atlantic. Follow Lloyds Road northwest for 1km back to Lizard at Beacon Terrace. Turn left and return to the start.

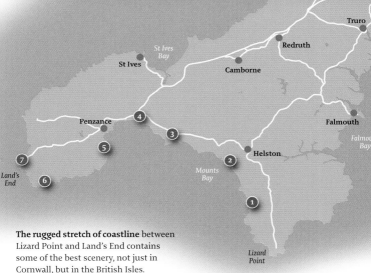

The rugged stretch of coastline between Lizard Point and Land's End contains some of the best scenery, not just in Cornwall, but in the British Isles.

The turquoise waters, steep cliffs and rich wildlife in and around Mullion Cove, Piskies Cove, Porthleven and Perranuthnoe are fantastic and the vistas extend along and across much of Mounts Bay, where sections of the coastline have been designated as Sites of Special Scientific Interest due to the importance of their geology and wildlife.

Cornwall's largest freshwater lake lies a little east of Porthleven; Loe Pool further emphasises the range of habitats to be found in Cornwall with cormorants, wigeon, teal, pochard, tufted duck, coot and shoveler all regularly spotted.

St Michael's Mount – arguably Cornwall's most iconic feature – sits a little offshore from the settlement of Marazion and is a landmark ideally viewed from Mousehole, the quintessential Cornish fishing village. After spending his honeymoon there, the Welsh poet Dylan Thomas described Mousehole as the 'loveliest village in England'.

The secluded Lamorna Cove was also the source of artistic inspiration, as it became a haven for the artists of the Newlyn School in the late 19th century.

Heading west, undisturbed places like Porthcurno and Porthgwarra nestle amidst a stunning landscape and provide more peaceful spots to walk in before reaching the bustling environs of Land's End.

Sennen Cove offers a quieter approach to England's most westerly point where you can enjoy the simpler sights – from the smallest lichen clinging to the cliffs to giant basking sharks gliding offshore.

Land's End from Sennen Cove ▶

South West to Land's End

Poldhu and Mullion Coves

Distance 7.25km **Time** 2 hours 15
Terrain minor roads, coastal and
countryside paths **Map** OS Explorer 103
Access bus from Helston to Mullion; free
car park at Mullion (donations welcome)

**The Lizard Peninsula's west coast is
studded with pretty beaches and
sheltered coves, all linked by craggy cliffs.
This walk, bookended by quiet roads and
paths, journeys above an exquisite stretch
of coastline to visit the stunning coves of
Poldhu and Mullion.**

Mullion is the largest village on the
Lizard. At its centre is the fine St Mellanus
Church, which dates from the 13th
century (though much of the present
building is from the 1500s) and is
dedicated to St Mellanus, the Bishop of
Rennes, who was born in Brittany in the
sixth century.

From Mullion car park, opposite the
16th-century Old Inn, turn right onto

Lender Lane (signposted for Poldhu) and
walk out of the village along pavement
and then roadside verge for just under
1km to Angrouse Court. Turn left onto a
rough road and continue past Angrouse
Farm and several houses.

Once past a house called Seven Pines
the road narrows to a track; beyond a gate,
this reaches Poldhu at the Marconi
Centre. On 12 December 1901 Guglielmo
Marconi, the pioneering Italian inventor,
successfully received the first Morse
signal transmission across the Atlantic
from Poldhu to Newfoundland. The
Marconi Centre opened on 12 December
2001 to commemorate this event.

Turn right onto a road and walk
downhill to Poldhu Beach, a popular surf
spot and equally enticing for a break.

Retrace your steps towards the Marconi
Centre but, just before this, bear right
onto the coast path. This climbs onto the
cliffs before leading southeast past a

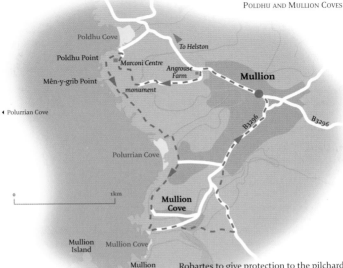

Poldhu Cove

To Helston

Poldhu Point

Marconi Centre

Angrouse Farm

Mullion

Mên-y-grib Point

monument

◄ Polurrian Cove

B3296

B3296

Polurrian Cove

0   1km

Mullion Cove

Mullion Island

Mullion Cove

Mullion Cliff

monument dedicated to Marconi above the shimmering waters of the bay. Once through a gap in a wall, fork right to follow the path on a gradual descent, branching right again just before a house to reach a junction. Turn right here to reach the golden sands of Polurrian Cove.

Cross a footbridge, then climb steep steps onto the great folded cliffs above the cove. At a road turn right and, after the last of several houses, go right onto a path, then right again where a road passes a hotel and car park. A steep path on the right descends to Mullion Cove and its small working harbour, which was developed between 1893 and 1895 and financed by local landowner and MP Lord

Robartes to give protection to the pilchard boats that sailed from here.

Turn left onto Nansmellyon Road (B3296), climbing steeply to Mullion Hill Farm and bearing right onto a public footpath and then right at a fork. A sustained ascent takes you past numerous houses to the top of a stony track. Go through the central of three gates, cross a stile and follow a field-edge path to meet the quiet Ghost Hill road.

Turn left to follow this downhill and, when it starts to climb, look for a public footpath on the right which shortcuts through woodland, across a footbridge and diagonally over a field to a stile onto Nansmellyon Road. Turn right and walk along the roadside into Mullion, keeping left onto Churchtown to reach the car park.

Porthleven and Penrose Estate

Distance 6.75km **Time** 2 hours
Terrain minor roads, coastal and
countryside paths **Map** OS Explorer 103
Access car park at Porthleven (parking
charge); bus from Helston to Porthleven

**The fishing village of Porthleven is the
start point for a varied route that makes
its way through Penrose Estate and above
Loe Pool, the largest natural freshwater
lake in Cornwall, before following a
stunning stretch of coastline.**

Porthleven Harbour is England's most
southerly port and was built in the early
19th century, primarily as a safe harbour
for boats caught in stormy seas, though it
was home to its own large fishing fleet.
Industries such as fishing and
boatbuilding helped the village to develop
around this time. It is thought the

derivation of Porthleven is either 'The
Smooth Port' or the 'Port of St Elvan', who
landed here in the 5th century to spread
the word of Christianity.

From Porthleven Harbour walk south
along Harbour Road and past the striking
clocktower of the Bickford-Smith Institute.
Today it is home to Porthleven Town
Council, but it was originally built in 1882
to house a scientific and literary institute,
having been gifted to the village by William
Bickford-Smith, a former MP for Truro.

Swing left onto Cliff Road, which rises
steadily away from the harbour with fine
views along Porthleven Sands. When the
road splits, go left and continue to climb
onto Shrubberies Hill and out of the
village. After just under 1km, you come to a
junction with the B3304.

Turn right here and go right again

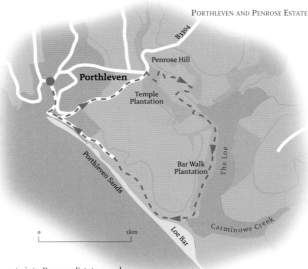

Porthleven

Penrose Hill

Temple
Plantation

B3304

Bar Walk
Plantation

The Loe

Porthleven Sands

Carminowe Creek

Loe Bar

0   1km

through a gate into Penrose Estate, much of which has been in the care of the National Trust since 1974. Now on estate roads, go left at a fork and continue through woodland to a T-junction. Turn right, then left to continue across a bridge and through lovely countryside to meet another estate road on the right.

Follow this as it curves left past houses and a walled garden to become a woodland track. This takes you on a meandering course through the grounds before veering right above the expanse of Loe Pool, where cormorants, wigeon, teal, pochard, tufted duck, coot and shoveler may be spotted at various times.

The track rises gently along the lake's western shore for 1km, leaving the estate through a gate above Loe Bar, a large shingle bank thought to have been formed

around the 12th century (though it may have its origins as far back as the last ice age) after storms blocked the Cober Valley from the sea.

Once past a large stone house, you can detour down to the beach by a track or just continue along a picturesque section of the South West Coast Path, heading northwest above the long finger of Porthleven Sands, with expansive views across Mounts Bay and south along the Lizard. After around 750m, the path zigzags steeply down to a small car park – cross this onto a single-track road and then go straight on along Highburrow as it leads downhill onto Loe Bar Road and back into Porthleven. At Cliff Road, retrace your steps to the harbour.

◀ Porthleven Harbour

Perranuthnoe to Prussia Cove

Distance 6.75km **Time** 2 hours
Terrain minor roads, coastal and
countryside paths **Map** OS Explorer 103
Access buses from Penzance and Helston
to Perranuthnoe; car park at Perranuthnoe
(parking charge)

**Rich in smuggling legend and lore, the
coves at the end of this walk are reached
by following the jagged coastline
southeast from Perranuthnoe, returning
on quiet roads and field paths.**

Documented evidence of Perranuthnoe,
which sits around 3km east of Marazion,
can be traced back to the Domesday survey
of 1086, when the village's population
consisted of eight smallholders, seven
villagers and three slaves.

From the village car park, turn left and

then left again onto a narrow road for
Prussia Cove. This turns right just before
a house and, after a few metres, right
again onto a rough track, which descends
towards the coast. Just before it swings
left, turn right onto a waymarked path,
then left onto a field-edge path.

Once through a gate, continue through
open countryside with views extending
along the Lizard. After another gate, the
gorse-lined path proceeds southeast to
Trevean Cove. At a fork, go right, carry on
through a gate and over two footbridges.
The path runs through hawthorn bushes,
crosses a stile and then leads down some
steps to skirt around Stackhouse Cove.

Once over another stile, the spiny
profile of Cudden Point lies ahead and,
after a steep pull, you are rewarded with a

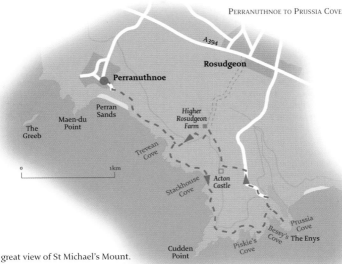

great view of St Michael's Mount. A right turn takes you onto Cudden Point's airy ridge; the coastline here is a Site of Special Scientific Interest due to the importance of its geology and wildlife.

Continuing on the coast path, the blue waters of Piskie's Cove soon come into view – piskies are Cornish fairies. Descend steeply past the cove, then climb steadily, keeping left at a fork. A steady drop takes you round Bessy's Cove and past an old thatched cottage. Go left at a fork to continue, then right onto a track and right again onto a narrow road to descend to Prussia Cove, which has strong links with smuggling, most famously with John Carter, the self-styled 'King of Prussia'.

Retrace your steps along the road and past the point where you joined it. After a scattering of houses and a public footpath on the left, the road swings sharp right.

Keep an eye out for another public footpath on the left, just after a metal gate.

Cross a stile here and go straight on along a field-edge path. Near the end of the field bear right, cross another stile and then follow another field path to the right of the houses at Acton Castle. Sweep right to a gate on the left. Beyond this turn right onto Trevean Lane, walk north and, just before Trevean Farm, turn left through a gate onto a path for Trevean Cove. After another gate, turn right and climb to a track, turning left here to continue to a three-way fork.

Take the central path and then turn right onto a field path, which returns to the outward path at Trevean Cove. Retrace your steps to Perranuthnoe.

◀ Piskie's Cove

Marazion and St Michael's Mount

Distance 5.25km **Time** 1 hour 45
Terrain minor roads, cyclepath, causeway
Map OS Explorer 103 **Access** buses from
Penzance and Helston to Marazion; car
park at Marazion (parking charge)

**Although Marazion's popularity is largely
down to being the jumping-off point for
the iconic St Michael's Mount, it is an
attractive destination in its own right.
This walk follows quieter lanes and roads
around the village before taking the
causeway (or ferry) to the island.**

Marazion claims to be one of Britain's
oldest towns and was known as Ictis
during Roman times. Trading seems to
have been central to its longevity (in
particular tin, with evidence of this
extending as far back as the Iron Age);
Marazion translates from the Cornish
Marghasbigan, meaning 'Little Market'.
Today its selection of shops and galleries
make this an interesting place to visit.

The village and surrounding area also
has its place in the legends of Jack the

Giant Killer, having long suffered the
attentions of Cormoran, a giant who lived
on St Michael's Mount and waded across
the water to devour livestock, during King
Arthur's reign. Local boy Jack was said to
have rowed out and lured Cormoran to his
death in a pit-trap, this being the first in a
series of giants slain by the plucky Cornish
lad in the traditional fairytale.

Facing the Godolphin Arms Hotel on
West End, turn right and follow the road
out of the village. Once past a large car park
bear right onto Green Lane, which then
sweeps to the right. Carry on along the
hedgerow-lined road, past the entrance of
a caravan park, before leaving it for Green
Lane West, a quiet narrow road (also
National Cycle Network Route 3) heading
northeast past several houses.

In due course the road reaches its end
beside an old cottage. Go left onto a path
(and cyclepath) and walk through
woodland below the A394. Exit the
woodland and follow the path, now
alongside the A394, until it drops down to

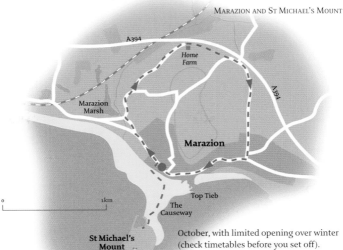

A394

Home
Farm

A394

Marazion
Marsh

Marazion

0   1km

Top Tieb

The
Causeway

**St Michael's
Mount**

a minor road (Gwallon Lane). Turn right and follow this back towards Marazion.

Gwallon Lane becomes Shop Hill once past Marazion Community Centre, and this descends to Turnpike Road. Turn right to enjoy great views of St Michael's Mount as you head back into Marazion via Fore Street and then into the village centre at The Square.

To walk to St Michael's Mount, return to the Godolphin Arms, going left down to the beach to cross the causeway. If you miss the causeway opening times, a regular ferry sails from Marazion, either from Chapel Rock, Top Tieb or Gwelva (depending on the tide). The island's harbour, sub-tropical gardens and castle make this a wonderful place to explore. The castle and gardens are open daily except Saturday between April and October, with limited opening over winter (check timetables before you set off).

The island is dedicated to St Michael who, according to Cornish legend, appeared to a group of fishermen in 495AD, standing on a rocky shelf on the Mount's western side. Since then it has been an important site of pilgrimage. In the 11th century, the island was granted to the Benedictine monks of Mont St Michel in France, and since then it has been used as a fortress (during the War of the Roses and the English Civil War of the mid-17th century, for example). As a busy port, it once had a population of around 200, plus three schools and pubs. In 1954 the St Aubyn Family, who had owned St Michael's Mount since the 17th century, gifted it to the National Trust whilst retaining a 999-year lease to live on and manage the island. To return to Marazion, take a ferry or cross the causeway back to the mainland.

Lamorna Cove from Mousehole

Distance 9.5km **Time** 3 hours
Terrain minor roads, coastal paths; tricky
and steep sections **Map** OS Explorer 103
Access bus from Penzance to Mousehole;
car park on outskirts of Mousehole
(parking charge)

**This out-and-back route between
Mousehole and Lamorna Cove contains
some awkward terrain – especially
between Penzer Point and Kemyel Crease
– where care is required. However, the
scenery alone makes it worth the effort.**

The route begins from Mousehole
(pronounced 'Mowzel'), described by Welsh
writer Dylan Thomas as 'the loveliest
village in England' (Thomas married Caitlin
McNamara in nearby Penzance in 1937).
Mousehole's history as a port extends back
to the 13th century – it was, for the next 300
years, the main fishing port in Mounts Bay.

In 1595, Spanish raiders razed Mousehole
and also attacked Paul, Penzance and

Newlyn in the only successful (albeit brief
and ultimately non-decisive) invasion of
English soil of the Anglo-Spanish War.
Point Spaniard, passed on this route, is a
reminder of the conflict, and in Merlyn
Rock, just north of this, history and myth
converge. According to Arthurian legend,
the wizard Merlin is said to have predicted
the invasion, saying: 'There shall land on
the Rock of Merlin/Those who shall burn
Paul, Penzance and Newlyn'. However,
there is no evidence of the prophecy being
recorded until after the raid.

From the picture-postcard Mousehole
Harbour walk south through the village,
veering right onto Mill Lane and then left
onto Chapel Street. A prolonged ascent
takes you up Raginnis Hill away from the
village centre. Where the gradient eases,
pass a row of cottages and turn left onto a
narrow road for the 'Coast Path'.

When the road forks, go right onto a
rough track. After several houses a path

◀ Lamorna Cove

continues between the hedgerows with views across Mounts Bay to the Lizard Peninsula. Initially good as it descends above Point Spaniard, the path becomes rougher and overgrown as the gradient steepens, hampering progress. Once above Penzer Point the trail drops steeply down steps, then runs southwest just above the rocky coastline, becoming awkward to cross at points, with short, steep descents and ascents and some boulders and overgrown vegetation to negotiate.

Once the path enters Kemyel Crease Nature Reserve it improves greatly. This little pocket of woodland, dominated by Monterey Pine, is cared for by the Cornwall Wildlife Trust which purchased it in 1974. In the early 20th century, the south-facing cliff slopes were terraced to prevent erosion and allow cultivation. Known as 'quillets', the terraced fields were divided by stone walls and planted with trees and shrubs, which provided shelter for crops and potatoes during the Second World War.

Beyond the reserve, an easy stroll continues along the coast and then a steep pull from Kemyel Point leads to a superb vista to St Michael's Mount and Tater Du Lighthouse. After a short descent the path heads northwest above Lamorna Cove,

across a rugged stretch of coast, to reach the small harbour.

A lovely sheltered spot, Lamorna Cove became a haven for artists from the late 19th century, particularly those of the Newlyn School who were attracted by the wonderful light and colour along the coast.

Retrace your steps to Mousehole, bearing in mind that there are a couple of steep ascents on the return journey.

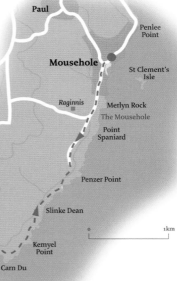

Porthcurno and Porthgwarra

**Distance 6km Time 1 hour 45
Terrain** minor roads, coastal and
countryside paths **Map** OS Explorer 103
Access limited bus service from Penzance
to Porthcurno; car park at Porthcurno
(parking charge)

**On the southwest tip of the Cornish coast,
the undisturbed villages of Porthcurno
and Porthgwarra are easily linked by
peaceful country paths and a sweep of
coastline, passing the famous open-air
Minack Theatre on the return.**

From Porthcurno car park, turn right
and follow the road past the Porthcurno
Telegraph Museum, which details
Porthcurno's role at the centre of
international cable communications
when it had the largest cable station in
the world. Such was Porthcurno's
importance in communication during the
Second World War that an underground
cable station was built for telegraph

apparatus in case of attack – the Tunnels
now house the main museum displays.

Once past some cottages turn sharp left
onto a public bridleway. At a fork keep
right and beyond a gate a track crosses a
field, then passes a farm. As it swings left
turn right through a gate, cross another
field track and go through a gate into the
grounds of the pretty St Levan's Church.
Follow a path around its front, exiting
through a gate onto a narrow road.

Go straight across onto a footpath for
Porthgwarra. Once across a footbridge
climb steadily between hedgerows to a
fork. Go right for a steep ascent to a field.
Keep to its right edge (with views
extending to the spiky Hella Point) as it
drops down to reach the rocky coast. The
route runs west, passing a waymarked path
on the left, which is used on the return.

As the path begins to descend towards
Porthgwarra, turn right up wooden steps
onto a waymarked path and follow this

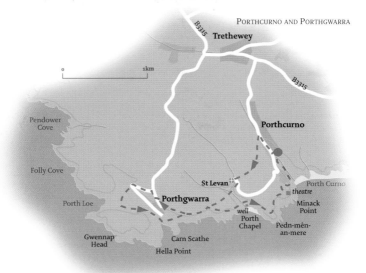

past a couple of houses to a junction.

Turn right onto a narrow road and then left to follow a minor road down towards Porthgwarra. As it swings left, go right through a gate and take a path downhill and over a footbridge, then climb to a road beside a large house. Turn left, cross a stile and take the road down to the village.

After a car park, swing left past Porthgwarra shop. Turn right onto a track, for Minack, then go left at a fork (right leads through a spectacular archway to the beach). Turn right at the next fork to climb steps onto a path, rejoining the outward path at the wooden steps. Carry straight on for around 250m to the waymark passed earlier.

Bear right to follow the path along gorse-covered cliffs, soon going down steps around Porth Chapel Bay and St Levan's Holy Well, which is still used for baptisms.

It is then a steep ascent to the rocky headland of Pedn-men-an-mere with its magnificent view across Porth Chapel Bay. Follow the cliff path for views along the pristine white sands of the National Trust-owned Porthcurno Beach, and pass through a gate beside the renowned open-air Minack Theatre. Since 1932, when the first audience clambered down the cliffpath to watch a performance of *The Tempest*, lit only by car headlamps, batteries and the whims of the moon, the theatre has staged hundreds of productions by companies around the world.

Turn left through the car park and, at a junction, go right and then left onto a narrow path. This zigzags steeply down towards Porthcurno Beach. Turn left onto another path, then go right at a fork and follow a wide track back to the car park.

◀ Porthcurno Beach   49

Sennen Cove to Land's End

Distance 4.25km **Time** 1 hour 15
Terrain coastal and countryside paths
Map OS Explorer 103 **Access** limited bus
service from Penzance to Sennen Cove;
car park at Sennen Cove (parking charge)

**Although only a mile or so from Land's
End, Sennen Cove could be a million miles
away. The walk follows a delightful stretch
of coastline, offering a quiet approach to
the tourist bustle on Land's End with
extensive views throughout.**

A popular spot for bathers and surfers,
Whitesand Bay stretches north in a great
arc from Sennen Cove harbour. This route,
however, heads west from the harbour.
Walk through the car park past the public
toilets; turn left onto a road, then climb

steps that sweep right and reach a
coastguard lookout post, a wild and
windswept spot, where a superb view
extends northeast along Whitesand Bay
and southwest towards Land's End and
Longships Lighthouse.

Waves and wind have shaped this
remarkable coastline into one of extremes
– from the wild weather, the great granite
cliffs and the sandy beaches to the array of
wildlife, right up from the smallest lichen
to the world's second largest fish (basking
sharks) that glide around these waters.

Bear left from the lookout onto a wide
path and, at a junction, turn right. Walk
above the spiky coastline, looking out on
an expanse of sea which remains unbroken
until the Isles of Scilly are reached, some

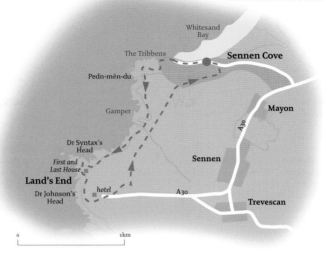

45km to the west. The path continues easily past several granite tors, weathered and eroded over many millennia, whilst thrift, sea campion and wild thyme cling to the clifftops.

A fairly steep climb then leads to a path on the right, which can be followed to Dr Syntax's Head – the most westerly point on Land's End – with its view to the incredible feat of engineering that is Longships Lighthouse, sitting almost 2km out to sea. The present structure dates from 1875 (it was automated in 1988) and replaced the original light, which had stood since 1795, guiding ships around these treacherous waters.

The range of wildlife found on the rocks and offshore is as impressive as the scenery – from shag, herring gull, great black-backed gull, razorbill and fulmar to common, bottlenose and risso dolphins, and even the occasional killer whale.

Follow the narrow road up to a hotel and several shops and continue to reach an access road at a car park. A path runs left of the road and, upon reaching a coach park, the road and path swing left to a junction.

Turn left onto a track (National Cycle Network Route 3) and follow this easily as it meanders north and then northeast, level at first, then making the gradual climb back to Sennen Cove after 1km.

Go straight on along the quiet street of Marias Lane, leaving it for a public footpath on the left when the road begins to lead downhill – this path drops steadily down to a narrow road at the village centre. Follow this back to the harbour.

Heading north, the Cornish coast begins to feel busier, especially at St Ives. Before you come to this, you cross some of Cornwall's most historic and economically important landscapes. Cape Cornwall, the village of St Just and the sheltered Kenidjack Valley all have their recent history indelibly linked with mining, and tangible evidence of the industry can be seen when walking here.

St Ives is regarded by many as the prettiest of all Cornish towns and there are several great walks here, including a tough coastal challenge to River Cove and a simple stroll around the town to visit St Nicholas Chapel, Tate St Ives and the Barbara Hepworth Museum.

The town is linked with the village of Carbis Bay by a wonderful section of the South West Coast Path. It will be hard to leave Carbis Bay's arc of golden sand behind, but the path continues from here to Lelant with stunning views along the way. A little inland rises Trencrom Hill, site of an Iron Age fort.

Wildlife comes to the fore in and around the dunes of Gwithian Towans and St Gothian Sands – curlew, sandpipers, ring ouzel, stonechat and dark green fritillary butterflies all thrive in the shadow of Godrevy Lighthouse, another of Cornwall's iconic structures.

A ragged and exposed coastline, as well as West Cornwall's largest area of woodland, can be enjoyed in and around Portreath and Tehidy, whilst the long golden stretch of Perran Sands is enjoyed on a walk that leaves from Holywell and visits St Piran's Cross, one of Cornwall's earliest Christian sites.

Newquay

Perran Bay

St Agnes Head

Truro

Redruth

St Ives Bay

St Ives

Camborne

Falmouth

Penzance

Land's End

Helston

Mounts Bay

St Ives and around

▼ St Ives from Smeaton's Pier

Kenidjack and Cape Cornwall

**Distance 8km Time 2 hours 30
Terrain** minor roads, coastal and
countryside paths **Map** OS Explorer 103
Access buses from Penzance to St Just;
car park on Market Street

**This walk travels between village, valley
and coast through one of Cornwall's most
historic mining landscapes and out to
dramatic Cape Cornwall – at one time
thought to be the English mainland's
most westerly point.**

St Just has been a bustling town since
Cornwall's mining boom of the 19th
century when it was the centre of mining
in the area. This is reflected in the
numerous engine houses and chimneys
that are passed on this walk.

From Market Square follow Church
Street past St Just Parish Church, then veer
left onto a lane, which heads downhill to
New Road. Turn left, follow a roadside
verge through Tregeseal and then
pavement through Nancherrow to the
B3306. Cross onto a narrow road, which
heads northwest into the historic
Kenidjack Valley. At one time there were
eight mines and a surprising concentration
of mills here. Thanks to the small river – a
comparative rarity on this stretch of coast
– the valley floor was littered with up to 50
waterwheels, leats, ponds and sluices.

After 750m a stony track continues
through the peaceful countryside. At a
National Trust sign for Kenidjack bear left,
follow a broad track past some old mine
buildings and after a chimney go left at a
fork. Beyond a gate, turn left, then left

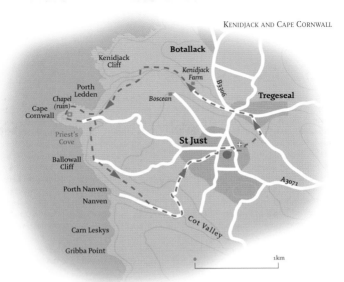

again after a second gate and cross a footbridge over a river. A path now travels along the valley floor, then veers left to zigzag onto cliffs above Kenidjack.

A high-level coast walk now proceeds southwest where stunning views extend to Cape Cornwall and Land's End. At a junction beside a cottage turn right and descend a track to the Cape Cornwall access road. Turn right and follow a path to the right of the road along a field edge. Cross a stile and, after a gap in a wall, bear right, then take a field path past St Helen's Oratory, one of the first Christian chapels in the west of Cornwall.

Crossing a stile at the field's right corner, go straight on along a path, then climb a path on the left onto the summit of Cape Cornwall, adorned by its 140-year-old

chimney stack – a remnant of the Cape's tin mine but now a navigational aid for ships.

Descend steeply to the access road and turn left. Just before a gate, go right down some steps towards Priest's Cove, then left at a junction, where a sharp climb leads to a stony track on the right. Take this as it climbs steeply onto a road. After about 20m go right onto a path opposite a trig point and descend southeast, past several closed mine buildings, into the Cot Valley.

At a minor road turn left and climb steeply through peaceful countryside for around 1km to return to St Just at Bosorne Road. Once past St Just Primary School walk left to Cape Cornwall Street. Go right and continue to Bank Square where a right turn takes you back to Market Square.

◀ Cape Cornwall

Wild side of St Ives

Distance 13km **Time** 4 hours 15
Terrain pavement, rough coastal paths
Map OS Explorer 102 **Access** regular trains
between St Erth, Lelant and St Ives on the
scenic St Ives Bay Line; several car parks in
St Ives (parking charges), but these are
very busy in summer and the Park & Ride
at Lelant Saltings is recommended

On this tougher walk between St Ives and
River Cove, a labyrinth of narrow, bustling
streets gives way to a rough, lonely stretch
of coast where the bare, rugged cliffs are
offset by heather heathland – a mass of
vibrant purple in July and August.

Wildflowers such as heath-spotted
orchids, thrift and sea campion thrive on
this stretch of granite coast, slow worms
and many species of butterfly populate the
heath, while colonies of kittiwakes and
great black-backed gulls nest on the cliffs
in spring and summer; year round you may
spot a buzzard soaring or kestrel hovering
above. Some short sections of the coastal
path are rough underfoot and can slow
progress considerably.

Start at St Ives Railway Station, above the
popular, sandy Porthminster Beach. Exit
right onto The Terrace (A3074), then walk
down Tregenna Hill and sweep right onto
High Street. At St Ives Parish Church, go
left and then right, drop down Lifeboat

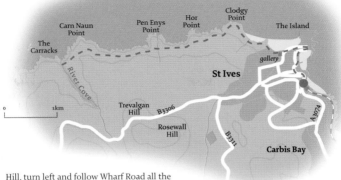

Hill, turn left and follow Wharf Road all the way around the harbour – the tourist hub of the town.

At Smeaton's Pier go left, climb Pier View onto Back Road East and then Back Road West, before passing the Tate St Ives and Porthmeor Beach, its more exposed aspect making it a favourite with surfers; there is a good view of St Nicholas Chapel here (see page 58). Beyond Porthmeor Bowling Club, a paved path passes a rocky headland and an elaborate stone shelter to meet a stony path. This rises steeply before dropping to a rocky bay and passing through a gate.

Keep right at a fork and continue to Clodgy Point, a rocky promontory with fine views along the coast. After the path swings left, go straight on at a first waymark and right at the next. From here, the walking becomes rougher underfoot.

Bear west, passing wild rocky coves and inlets. Keep right at a fork. A steep climb up Hellesveor Cliff takes you to a junction above Hor Point, where you turn right for a high-level clifftop walk, the path now much improved – though with short, sharp ups and downs to negotiate.

Carry on along the heather heathland above Pen Enys Point, continuing along part of the Trevalgan Farm Trail after a gate – ahead on the horizon sit the remains of a tin mining engine house. The undulations become softer, with a gradual ascent to gain Carn Naun Point and a trig point with wide-ranging views southwest towards Zennor Head and inland to Rosewall Hill and Trendrine Hill.

Dropping gently at first, the path steepens to reach River Cove, where you can sit and watch waterfalls cascade into the sea or look for grey seals a short distance out on The Carracks.

To return, retrace your steps to St Ives. The walking is just as tough, but the views extending to Godrevy Lighthouse and, on a clear day, some 48km to Trevose Head, make it a real joy.

◀ Porthmeor Beach

St Ives and the Island

Distance 6.5km **Time** 1 hour 45
Terrain pavement, coastal paths
Map OS Explorer 102 **Access** regular trains
between St Erth, Lelant and St Ives on the
scenic St Ives Bay Line; several car parks in
St Ives (parking charges), but these are
very busy in summer and the Park & Ride
at Lelant Saltings is recommended

St Ives is one of Cornwall's most attractive
towns, its tight, busy streets bordered by
a string of beautiful beaches. At its
northern tip is the rounded hump of the
Island and the remains of St Nicholas
Chapel. Nearby are the Tate St Ives and
Smeaton's Pier. This walk visits them all.

From St Ives Railway Station, exit right
onto The Terrace (A3074), then walk down
Tregenna Hill before turning left onto the
B3306. Climb gradually away from the town
centre for around 750m, straight over three
mini-roundabouts, to Carnellis Road. Go

right onto this quiet street, which soon
becomes Alexandra Place, before veering
right along Alexandra Road.

Turn left onto Burthallan Lane to pass
several houses and the Garrack Hotel. After
the lane narrows, a rougher track continues
towards the coast. When it forks at Higher
Burthallan House go right onto a path and
descend gently over heath, eventually
dropping down onto the South West Coast
Path. Carry straight on to round the rocky
Clodgy Point. After a gate, continue past a
rocky bay with a steep pull leading onto
higher ground and a lovely view along
Porthmeor Beach to St Nicholas Chapel.

Beyond an elaborate stone shelter, a paved
path leads past Porthmeor Bowling Club
onto a pavement, following Porthmeor Hill
to the excellent Tate Gallery. Opened in

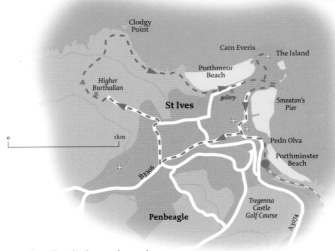

1993, the gallery displays modern and contemporary art. Also managed by the Tate is the nearby Barbara Hepworth Museum – Hepworth spent much of her life living and working in St Ives.

Bear right and then left onto Back Road West and Back Road East, before turning left at Island Square onto Island Road and continuing through a car park to the Island. During prehistoric times the Island was literally that at high tides. Known originally as Pendinas, meaning 'Fortified Headland', it is connected to the mainland by an isthmus and its crest is a great vantage point for viewing the bay.

Turn left at an information board and climb a path up to St Nicholas Chapel. St Nicholas is the patron saint of sailors and this chapel has been a place of worship for many centuries, although there is no

record as to when it was built. During the 18th century it was used as a lookout post for excise officers and from 1879 as a store for the war office.

Returning to Island Square, turn left, follow Back Road East onto Pier View, then go down to Smeaton's Pier, where you are rewarded with views of St Ives. The pier was built by renowned civil engineer John Smeaton between 1767 and 1770. At its entrance is St Leonard's Chapel, where fishermen prayed before they went to sea.

Walk along The Wharf and at a slipway bear right onto Fore Street. Follow this tight, cobbled street, keeping left at a fork. Once across Lifeboat Hill turn right beside St Ives Parish Church onto High Street, then left onto Tregenna Hill and climb back to the railway station.

◂ St Nicholas Chapel

Carbis Bay, St Ives and The Steeple

Distance 8.25km **Time** 2 hours 45
Terrain pavement, coastal paths
Map OS Explorer 102 **Access** regular trains
between St Erth, Lelant, St Ives and Carbis
Bay on the St Ives Bay Line; car park at
Carbis Bay Railway Station (parking charge)
or use the Park & Ride at Lelant Saltings

Linking Carbis Bay with St Ives is a lovely
predominantly wooded section of the
South West Coast Path. It runs above the
coast with fine views of the surrounding
scenery. Heading back into Carbis Bay,
a quiet road climbs to the 18th-century
Knill's Monument.

Carbis Bay only established itself as a
village after the railway line arrived in the
late 19th century, bringing with it a tourist
boom – the Carbis Bay Hotel dates from
1894. Prior to this, tin mining and fishing
were the main industries. Many of author
Rosamund Pilcher's novels are set here.

Walk through Carbis Bay Railway Station

car park onto a lane, bear right onto a
public footpath and descend gently
through woodland. At a fork go right and,
once across a footbridge, take a sharp right
and follow the road sloping down beneath
a railway viaduct.

Keep left past the Carbis Bay Hotel,
which sits above the beautiful Carbis Bay
beach, then climb steeply up steps onto a
wooded path. A steady climb leads above
the coast and crosses the railway line via a
bridge. Continue high above the crystal-
clear waters of Carbis Bay and onto Hain
Walk beside a path for Knill's Monument.

Follow the road past several houses for
250m, then turn right onto a rough track,
which descends steeply onto a narrow
road. Walk along here and, as it veers left,
carry straight on along a path to a junction.
Turn right and walk down a path to cross
the railway bridge, turn right and drop
down into St Ives at Porthminster Beach.

After crossing the beach, head away from

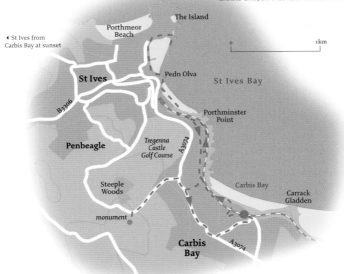

◄ St Ives from
Carbis Bay at sunset

it on the aptly named Warren, a narrow road lined with terraced houses. When this veers left, carry straight on along Pendola Walk to St Ives Lifeboat Station. Go straight on and follow Wharf Road (where there are plenty of pubs and restaurants) to the sandy beach at Smeaton's Pier.

Retrace your steps to Porthminster Beach. After crossing back over the railway bridge, climb a steep path, then go straight on at a crossroads onto Hain Walk. This soon returns to the outward-bound route and back to the signpost for Knill's Monument.

Bear right and climb a steep path, eventually passing through a gate onto

Wheal Margery. Turn right and, on reaching the A3074, go right. Once past the Cornish Arms turn left onto Higher Tregenna Road, then left again onto Steeple Lane. This narrow road climbs steadily for around 750m in distance to a path on the left that leads to the 15m-high Knill's Monument, also known locally as The Steeple. It was built as a mausoleum in 1782 by John Knill, a local collector of customs and the mayor of St Ives in 1767. His wish was to be buried here, but having died in London in 1811 he was instead buried in Holburn.

Retrace your steps to the A3074 and turn right into Carbis Bay. At Boskerris Road turn left to return to the railway station.

Tors of Trencrom Hill

Distance 3km **Time 1 hour**
Terrain hill paths, minor roads
Map OS Explorer 102 Access free National Trust car park at base of Trencrom Hill (donations welcome); nearest train station at St Erth, 4km away

Although rising to only around 170m, Trencrom Hill, near Lelant Downs, stands proud of the flatter surrounding landscape, and the summit of this ancient hillfort has one of Cornwall's finest panoramic views. Good paths traverse the hill with quiet scenic roads also featuring on this lovely little walk.

Begin from the small National Trust car park, which is around 1km west of Lelant Downs, on the right of a narrow road leading to Cripplesease. Take the gate at the back of the car park onto a path, which immediately begins to climb up the open southern side of Trencrom Hill (also known as Trecrobben Hill), scattered with large granite boulders.

It is a short but steady pull to gain the flat expansive summit where the reward is an excellent view. Two of Cornwall's most iconic buildings – the medieval castle on St Michael's Mount on the south coast and Godrevy Lighthouse on the north – are visible, and the view along this coastline stretches northeast from the broad sweep of Hayle Sands to Trevose Head.

The summit is littered with large granite tors, blocks which formed over several million years as they contained fewer faults and so weathered at a much

slower pace than the surrounding rock. An axe head was found on the slopes of Trencrom Hill dating back some 5500 years, and the outlook makes it apparent why this was later, during the Iron Age, chosen as a hillfort.

From the summit take the path that runs to the left of the first large granite tor. Descend towards another tor, but just before you reach this take the left branch at a fork (right leads up onto the tor) and descend northwest towards the scattering of houses at Trencrom. Drop down past another tor, going left here to continue to a crossroads at a stone marker (signposted 'Horse Track'). Turn right, before taking the left option at a fork to follow the path eastwards as

it traverses the lower slopes of Trencrom Hill. It swings right to another track, where you go left and descend to a gate.

Once through the gate, turn right onto a minor road a little east of Trencrom's houses. This leads through peaceful countryside with views towards Cornwall's north coast, before beginning a gradual descent, skirting some woods and then dropping down through trees to the outskirts of Lelant Downs.

Turn right and right again to take the unmarked Cripplesease road (which is quiet, though you still need to keep an eye out for traffic) for the final 800m or so, climbing steadily back to the car park.

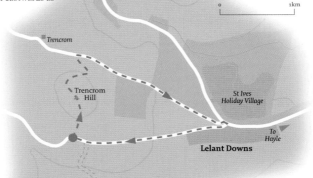

To
Carbis Bay

0   1km

Trencrom

Trencrom
Hill

St Ives
Holiday Village

To
Hayle

Lelant Downs

◀ Mounts Bay
from Trencrom Hill

Carbis Bay from Hayle Estuary

Distance 6.25km **Time** 1 hour 45
Terrain minor roads, golf course path,
coastal paths **Map** OS Explorer 102
Access regular trains from St Erth and
St Ives to Lelant on the St Ives Bay Line
– a stop must be requested when
boarding train; car park at Lelant Railway
Station (parking charge) or use the Park &
Ride at Lelant Saltings

Lelant Railway Station is the start point
for this simple walk that follows good
paths and quiet roads into Carbis Bay and
coastal paths on the return. Beautiful
views stretch across St Ives Bay and along
the golden expanse of Hayle Sands, with
plenty of wildlife-spotting opportunities.

Before setting out from the station, it is
worth taking a moment to look across
Hayle Estuary, the most westerly estuary
in Britain and an internationally
renowned RSPB reserve. While early
summer is the time of least activity on

the reserve, it has been known to attract
up to 18,000 birds in winter, when it is
possible to see teal and wigeon in their
thousands on the mudflats; in spring, it is
a migratory stop-off for waders such as
oystercatchers, dunlins, whimbrels,
greenshanks and bar-tailed godwits, while
autumn brings more waders still.

Cross Green Lane and climb Station Hill,
turning right onto Church Road. Walk
along here for 500m, sweeping left onto
Church Lane just before St Uny Church.
After another 300m turn right into West
Cornwall Golf Club. Follow the drive past
the clubhouse and through a car park,
then turn left onto a public footpath.

This track and then an indistinct grassy
path lead you northwest, between two
fairways, before bearing left through
gorse. Turn right to pass the 17th tee and
drop down to cross a track onto a narrow
path, where you shortly branch left. Once
through a gate, the path climbs gently

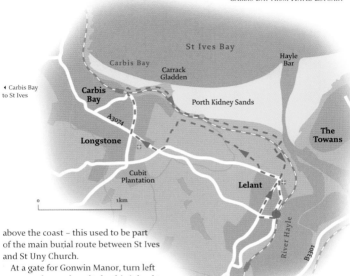

St Ives Bay

Carbis Bay

Hayle Bar

◀ Carbis Bay to St Ives

Carrack Gladden

Carbis Bay

Porth Kidney Sands

The Towans

A3074

Longstone

Cubit Plantation

Lelant

River Hayle

B3301

0   1km

above the coast – this used to be part of the main burial route between St Ives and St Uny Church.

At a gate for Gonwin Manor, turn left onto another path and take this inland to Longstone. Turn left to follow a road back to Church Lane, where you turn right and then right again onto the A3074 leading into Carbis Bay.

Go right down Porthrepta Road and, once across the bridge at Carbis Bay Railway Station, turn right onto a path for Lelant, going down steps towards Carbis Bay's long arc of sand. More steps climb away from the beach, the path now heading east along a superb stretch of coast with views of Godrevy Lighthouse.

Where the path forks, take the right branch; once up a steep flight of steps, a gradual ascent continues through hedgerows to a junction. Turn left and drop steadily along another path above

the clear waters at Porth Kidney Sands. A straightforward section runs left of a railway line, through grassland and alongside dunes. Although lacking the far-reaching views, the landscape is softer with lots of wildflowers to look out for during spring and summer.

Once past a level crossing, continue to a railway bridge. Turn right over this and follow the path alongside West Cornwall Golf Course. At a junction turn right, follow another path onto a lane and pass the distinctive St Uny Church to return to Church Road. Turn left onto Green Lane to take this narrow road back to the station.

St Gothian Sands Nature Reserve

Distance 5.25km **Time** 1 hour 30
Terrain coastal paths **Map** OS Explorer 102
Access car park at Gwithian Towans
(parking charge)

**This walk begins from Gwithian Towans,
the northern extremity of a stretch of
sand that extends some 5km southwest to
the outflow of the River Hayle. Good paths
cross St Gothian Sands Nature Reserve
and follow cliffs to reach Godrevy Point,
protected by a landmark lighthouse.**

Gwithian and St Gothian Sands are both
named after St Gothian, the patron saint of
good fortune on the sea. Records show
that a church was built here in 490AD
whilst ancient relics of St Gothian were
uncovered from the beach and dunes
during the early part of the 19th century
before being reclaimed by the sand. Bronze

Age artefacts have also been discovered,
confirming that people were living here
around 5000 years ago.

Start from Gwithian Towans car park
with the beach to your left – you're likely
to find yourself in the company of surfers
at most times of year, such is Gwithian's
popularity. Follow a gravel path to a
lifeguard lookout post, sweeping right
before turning left onto another path
which continues through Gwithian
Towans (*Towans* is the Cornish word for
dunes) to a fork. Take the left branch and
make your way into St Gothian Sands Local
Nature Reserve.

At a slate marker take the right fork,
going left at the next marker, then right at
a fork to continue through a site where
sand used to be extracted. After this
stopped, sandbanks and ponds were

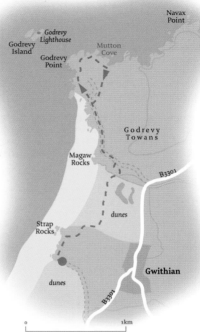

◀ Godrevy Lighthouse at dusk

created and because of the diversity of the wildlife found here it was designated a Site of Special Scientific Interest – curlew, sandpiper, dunlin, ring ouzel, stonechat and meadow pipit are a small selection of the birds that may be seen at various times.

Keep to the left of a pond, bearing right at the far end and then left through an opening in the sandbanks. Cross a footbridge over the Red River (so named because it was once stained red by the tin residue from mines upstream), turning left to climb steps and walk through a car park. Turn left onto a path marked for Portreath, which heads north, to the left of an access road and above the rocky coastline, towards Godrevy Point.

Once you have passed two more car parks bear right at a waymark, then left at a fork. Beyond a granite stile is a final gradual climb to Godrevy Point, where there are superb views across the water to Carbis Bay and St Ives, as well as to the iconic 26m-high Godrevy Lighthouse, standing atop Godrevy Island, just short of a reef called the Stones, site of many shipwrecks. The lighthouse was built in 1859, five years after a steamer called *The Nile* was wrecked here, claiming all life on board. In spring, this treacherous spot is blanketed in sea thrift, primrose and heather.

Continue around the headland, dropping down to cliffs above Mutton Cove, where at lower tides a colony of grey seals may be spotted – do not descend into the cove as it is dangerous and you might startle the seals. Instead turn right onto a wide track, skirt around a wooden barrier and return to the outward path beside a car park. Retrace your steps to the start.

Portreath and Tehidy Country Park

Distance 7.5km **Time** 2 hours 15
Terrain coastal and woodland paths,
minor roads **Map** OS Explorer 104
Access bus from Redruth to Portreath; car
park at Portreath (parking charge)

**This varied route leaves from the village of
Portreath and follows a dramatic section
of coastline before travelling through
Tehidy Country Park, the largest area of
woodland in West Cornwall.**

Portreath's development can be traced
back to 1760 when the existing harbour
was built to allow smaller vessels to dock
safely. It was subsequently expanded as
the demand for coal to power the local
mines grew. The construction of the
Poldice to Portreath tramroad in 1809,
where horses transported the coal, and the
arrival of the railway in Portreath in 1837
helped the village to grow.

From the car park turn right, cross a

bridge, then go right onto Battery Hill for a
steep climb above Portreath with views
across the harbour. Walk down to the
bottom of the road, turn left onto a path for
Gwithian and go through a gate. Take the
left path and climb steeply over Western
Hill onto the cliffs, which form a barrier
along the coast to Godrevy Lighthouse.

Turn left, follow the exposed cliff path
southwest, high above the coast. Beyond a
gate continue past the collapsed sea cave
of Ralph's Cupboard, where a spectacular
fin of rock juts out to sea. The 'cupboard' is
said to be named either after a smuggler
who hid his contraband here or the giant
Wrath who devoured passing ships,
returning to store his bounty in the former
cave. When seafarers started to avoid the
area, he hurled boulders at them and these
can be seen littering this stretch of coast.

After a while, steps drop steeply to cross a
footbridge, with a stiff pull and then zigzags

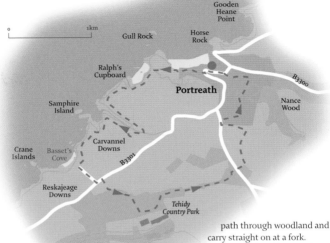

0 _____ 1km

Gooden
Heane
Point

Gull Rock

Horse
Rock

Ralph's
Cupboard

B3300

Portreath

Samphire
Island

Nance
Wood

Crane
Islands

Basset's
Cove

Carvannel
Downs

B3301

Reskajeage
Downs

Tehidy
Country Park

Oak
Wood

to return to the hillside at Carvannel
Downs. After another steep descent and re-
ascent the incline eases for a lovely high-
level walk to a car park at Basset's Cove.

Go left and take the rough road inland to
the B3301. Turn left, branching right after
30m to follow a path over a stile into
Tehidy Country Park. With more than 250
acres of woodland, it was, until 1916, in the
hands of the Bassets, one of Cornwall's
most powerful families, for 700 years. They
brought much employment to the area,
especially during the 19th century, and
when Sir Francis Basset died in 1835 20,000
people attended his funeral.

Go straight on at a crossroads, follow a
path through woodland and
carry straight on at a fork.

Continue to a T-junction, turning
left to follow a broad track to another
junction where you go left again. At the
next fork, keep left for East Lodge through
some pine trees and along the left edge of
a golf course. Take the left branch at a fork
to reach East Lodge car park.

From the car park cross the road and
follow the Portreath Mining Trail to the
outskirts of Portreath. Turn left at a
junction and follow this to the road. Turn
right, then left at a mini-roundabout and
after the road swings right, turn left
through a gate and follow the road past
Feadon Farm onto a path, which heads
down through woodland. Go left at a
junction, then left again to follow
Glenfeadon Terrace under a railway arch.
Keep left on a path to return to the start.

◀ Cliffs near Portreath

St Piran's pilgrimage

Distance 12km **Time** 3 hours 30
Terrain coastal and countryside paths,
minor roads **Map** OS Explorer 104
Access car park at Holywell (parking
charge for non-National Trust members)

**The landscape around Holywell, near
Newquay, is connected with St Piran, the
patron saint of tin miners and, to many,
the patron saint of Cornwall. This walk
visits a site closely associated with St
Piran, as well as taking in the beautiful
Perran Beach to the north of Perranporth.**

Leaving the National Trust car park at
Holywell Beach, turn right to follow the
road past St Piran's Inn, cross a bridge, then
turn right onto a surfaced path. Follow this
and then a narrow road southeast through
Holywell Bay Holiday Park.

At a whitewashed house, bear right onto
a wooded path for Cubert and Ellenglaze. In
a while, cross a footbridge, continuing
through pleasant countryside beyond a
gate. A rough road is soon picked up, which
passes through Ellenglaze to a junction.

Go straight on through a gate onto a path
for Trebisken and follow the right edge of a
field through a gate onto a wooded path.
After another gate cut diagonally across a
field, exiting via a stile at its right corner
onto another field path. Beyond a gate, a
wooded path approaches Trebisken, but
just before a narrow road turn right
through a gate to drop down through more
woodland and cross a footbridge.

Bear right and after another gate the
path crosses open countryside to the right
of woodland, reaching a minor road near

◄ Perran Beach

Mount. Turn right, walk for 1.5km (watch out for traffic) past Gear Farm, then take the second gate on the right opposite a side road for Rose.

A path swings right to an indistinct fork. Go right, then left when the path splits again. Keep straight on at a crossroads where a clearer path descends to another fork. Take the right branch. Continue to a waymark, keep left, climb gently to the next waymark, and go right to reach St Piran's Cross – one of only two three-holed crosses in Cornwall. Nearby are the remains of a church, thought to have been built by the Normans in the 12th century.

Walk west along a path, which swings left to a footbridge. Cross this, then go right at a fork and continue to St Piran's Oratory, which was founded around the 6th century by St Piran and is said to be one of the first places of Christian worship in Britain.

Continue up and over Penhale Sands before dropping down onto Perran Beach. The dunes here are thought to be over 5000 years old and have been used for agriculture, mining and religious worship.

Directly south from here is Perranporth, where St Piran spent much of his life, now a lively town with a popular family beach and a uniquely sited bar and restaurant on the sands. Head north along the sand to its very end and bear right onto the South West Coast Path. After a short, steep climb bear left at a fork, then left again onto a path to round Ligger Point, eventually gaining a broad, fenced track at Penhale Camp. This soon narrows to a path, which rounds Penhale Point. Drop down to Holywell Beach and, once through a gate, follow a sandy path back to the start.

71

The paths around Newquay offer simple, relaxed walking and pass some of the town's most interesting buildings. In sharp contrast is the jagged coastline of Bedruthan Steps – a favourite location for many visitors. The Steps have been shaped over millions of years and bottlenose dolphins are a common sight here.

Other notable spots include Rumps Point, which is an important breeding ground for puffins and gannets, as well as being the site of an Iron Age fort. Stepping even further back in time, the rounded summit of Brea Hill, near Rock, is the site of several Bronze Age tumuli.

A very rugged and tough section of coastal walking links Port Quin and Port Isaac, which is best known for being the location of the television series *Doc Martin*, whilst gentler walking can be found by following the River Camel at Wadebridge. The river reaches the sea at Padstow

where wading birds and wildflowers can be seen along the Camel Estuary.

Cornwall's impressive geology is clearly evident at the secluded Crackington Haven, with Cambeak providing views along the coast towards Bude and Northcott Mouth where more interesting geological formations can be found.

The Cornwall/Devon border is approached on reaching the little settlement of Morwenstow.

Newquay and the north coast

▼ Polzeath from Brea Hill

Newquay and Fistral Bay

Distance 8km **Time** 2 hours 15
Terrain coastal paths, pavement
Map OS Explorer 104 **Access** several car
parks in Newquay (parking charges);
Newquay is well served by public
transport from across Cornwall

**Newquay is known as a surfer's paradise,
but this walk shows that the town has
so much more to boast about – two rocky
headlands, a lovely sandy beach, an
historic harbour and interesting buildings.**

Originally known as Towan Blystra,
the name Newquay came into use during
the 15th century when a 'new quay' was
built; the present harbour dates from 1834
and when the railway arrived in 1876 it
opened up new trade opportunities as well
as heralding a boom in tourism, with
visitors drawn to Newquay's famed
sandy beaches.

From the harbour climb the steep
South Quay Hill before turning right onto
Fore Street. Walk through the town, then
make a right and go down North Quay
Hill. At a fork, go right and left at the
following fork. A narrow road leads onto
a coast path, which bears left up steps.
When it splits, keep right up more steps
onto King Edward Crescent.

Turn right to reach the distinctive Huer's
Hut and a fine view across Newquay Bay.
The hut dates from the 14th century and is
named after the Huer who would raise a
call when shoals of pilchards were sighted
in the bay.

Bear right just after the Huer's Hut to
follow the path above the coastline. When

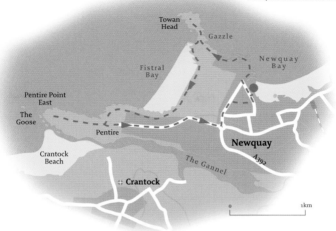

you reach a narrow road, turn right and cross a car park, passing the Old Lifeboat House, which was built in 1899 and in use until 1934, during which time 142 lives were saved. Newquay's first lifeboat, *The Joshua*, arrived in 1860, pulled by six horses.

Climb steeply onto Towan Head, which is topped with a distinctive hexagonal shelter giving views all along the coast.

Retrace your steps past the lifeboat house to take the second path on the right. This leads towards Fistral Beach, where some of the world's best surfing can be enjoyed. Once past some shops and cafés follow the path from the left corner of a car park. Running between the golf course and Fistral Beach, it can get a little overgrown, but improves when it drops left onto another path which eventually leads to Esplanade Road.

Turn right and walk past several hotels onto a rougher road, which rises steadily alongside some houses, then sweeps left to Pentire Avenue. Turn right, cross a small car park and take the path onto Pentire Point East – another fine vantage point.

Returning to Pentire Avenue, follow the pavement for 1km to meet Pentire Road. Cross Esplanade Road, passing around a barrier to take a path running parallel to Pentire Road. Once through an area of grassland the path drops down through a gate beside the pretty little Atlantic Road Cemetery.

Atlantic Road takes you to a junction where you branch left onto Tower Road. At Hope Terrace turn right and follow this onto Trevena Terrace and then Alma Place. Turn left onto Fore Street, then right onto South Quay Hill. From here it's a short stroll back down to the harbour.

◀ Towan Head

Bedruthan Steps and Porth Mear

Distance 7.5km **Time** 2 hours
Terrain coastal and countryside paths,
minor road **Map** OS Explorer 106
Access regular buses from Padstow
and Newquay stop at Carnewas car park
road end; car park at Carnewas (parking
charge for non-National Trust members)

**Bedruthan Steps is one of Cornwall's
'must see' destinations for walkers,
popular since Victorian times for their
wave-swept drama. These amazing stacks
have been shaped over millions of years,
the softer rock around them having been
battered and eroded away.**

Good paths hug the coastline to reach
Porth Mear, where you then head inland
through a conservation area and back to
Carnewas. The landscape here has been

inhabited for many millennia, with several
Iron Age and Bronze Age sites nearby. The
National Trust manages Carnewas and
there's a shop and tearoom here. During
the 19th century mining was important in
this area, with copper, lead and iron being
extracted from the cliffs. The tearoom and
shop were once mine buildings.

Take the path between the tearoom and
shop. Where the path splits take the right
branch, go left at the next fork and then
right at a junction. Follow the clifftop path
northwards, enjoying a great view of
Bedruthan Steps. A tale that first appeared
in the late 19th century claimed the name
originated from a legendary giant,
Bedruthan, who used the stacks to make a
shortcut across the bay, but it is more
likely that it refers to a staircase cut into

the cliff – before being later applied to the stacks and, more generally, the beach.

Each of the sea stacks that form the Steps has a name, including Queen Bess Rock, named in Victorian times for its likeness to Elizabeth I (though 'she' has since lost her head), Pendarves Island and Samaritan, after a cargo vessel wrecked here in 1846.

At a cobbled path turn left and go down some steps past a viewpoint, then climb steadily back onto the cliffs and past the prehistoric remains of Redcliff Castle.

Carnewas is soon left behind, with the path then continuing across Park Head. Keep your eyes peeled for bottlenose dolphins out in the bay. After a while, the path runs between a fence and a wall and then through a gate. Carry on to pass a gate on the right at Pentire Steps (for the return journey) and follow the grassy path a little way away from the cliff edge.

In due course pass through a gap in a wall and when the path forks go left and make your way towards the headland of Park Head. Turn right at a fork beside a memorial cairn. The path hugs the cliffs and drops down past High Cove to Porth Mear, where a wonderful view extends to Trevose Head.

Go down towards a small beach and, once through a gate, continue inland through a little valley, a conservation area with plenty of flowers and wildlife to look

out for. Beyond a gate, a steep path crosses a field, goes through another gate and then passes around the back of Pentire Farm. After the next gate bear left onto a narrow road and follow this to reach the car park for Park Head.

Go through the gate opposite the car park and follow the fenced path along the field edges to return to the outward-bound path at Pentire Steps. Turn left and retrace your steps to Carnewas, enjoying the views to Newquay.

Trevone to Trevose Head

Distance 11.25km **Time** 3 hours 45
Terrain coastal paths with steps
Map OS Explorer 106 **Access** car park at
Trevone (parking charge)

Trevose Head juts out into the Atlantic
on Cornwall's north coast, a few miles
west of Padstow, and is an important
breeding ground for fulmar, guillemot
and razorbill. A wild and windswept
stretch of coastline runs northwest from
the village of Trevone past Cataclews
Point and Mother Ivey's Bay to reach
Trevose Head Lighthouse. Harlyn Bay is
popular with surfers, particularly when
the wind whips in from the sea.

Turn right from the Trevone Bay car park
onto Trevone Road and walk through the
village, bearing right onto a coastal path

when the road forks at West View. Follow
this along the rocky coast, turning left at a
waymark through a gate, then right along a
field-edge path.

After a gate, the path carries on along the
cliffs past the dramatic Newtrain Bay
before arriving at the golden sands of
Harlyn Bay. Drop right down steps just
before a car park, cross the sand, then
come off the beach beside a stone bridge.
Cross the bridge over a stream, then
immediately turn right onto a waymarked
path. Head west along the sandy beach
and, once past a white house which sits on
cliffs above the beach, turn left and climb a
set of steps.

Go right where a path hugs the coastline.
Beyond a gate the path bears right at a
house, passes through another gate and

◀ View of Trevone

crosses a stile before travelling around Cataclews Point which has good views extending from Harlyn Bay eastwards towards Stepper Point with thrift, sea campion and English stonecrop clinging to the surrounding cliffs during spring and early summer.

After another gate, go down and then up some steps to follow a path which then runs to the right of a caravan park. More steps drop down to an entrance for the park. Cross a narrow road here, turn right onto a fenced path and take this past a house to a junction. Go right and follow the path around Mother Ivey's Bay, with its

prominent lifeboat station and the stacks of Merope Rocks at its northern tip.

Cross two stiles at a large house, turn left onto a narrow road and then immediately go right where the coastal path continues, crossing a stile. Carry straight on over a road, then over another stile and follow a field-edge path across open countryside, eventually returning to the clifftop path.

Follow this a short distance west to Trevose Head Lighthouse, built in 1847, with craggy coastal views extending south towards Newquay. From Trevose Head retrace your steps to Trevone and the start.

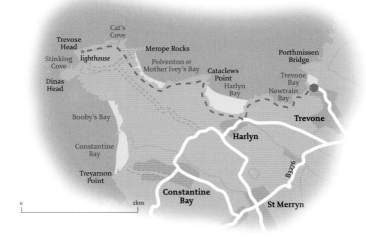

Padstow, Stepper Point and Trevone

Distance 11.5km **Time** 4 hours
Terrain minor roads, coastal and
countryside paths **Map** OS Explorer 106
Access regular buses from Bodmin to
Padstow; car park on Riverside, Padstow
(parking charge)

**Padstow stands on the Camel Estuary, an
Area of Outstanding Natural Beauty. The
surrounding sandbanks, reedbeds and
saltmarsh abound with wading birds and
wildflowers. The estuary's soft fringes
contrast with the dramatic, windswept
cliffs that run from Stepper Point to the
quiet village of Trevone, where quiet
paths and roads return to Padstow.**

The town of Padstow is a lively fishing
port, but it was once a major trading and
shipbuilding centre. It was also from here
that many Cornish families emigrated to
America and Australia. During medieval
times Padstow was granted a 'right of
sanctuary', which allowed criminals to
remain safe from arrest – something that
continued until the Reformation.

From Padstow Harbour follow West
Quay right onto North Quay. At a sign for
Hawker's Cove bear left and take a path
along the coast, passing a large memorial
cross and enjoying the views along the
Camel Estuary.

Keep north along the path, which soon
heads a little inland. Cross two stiles, then
turn right at a junction onto a rough
track. Branch left onto another path and
beyond a gate go down steps over a
footbridge, then straight on up another
set of steps.

A right turn leads back to the coast and
past Harbour Cove. Bear left at a fork,
make a right at the next junction, then
right again at a Trevone Bay sign. Once
past a couple of houses make a right turn
onto a road which passes through a gate,
and follow the path as it climbs steadily
away from Hawker's Cove, the gradient

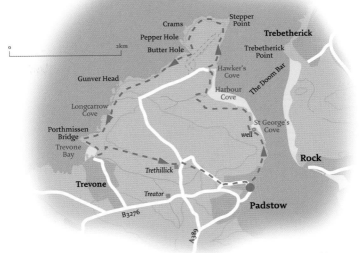

only easing when above Stepper Point.

Go through a gate here, cross a stile, then fork right (left leads to a lookout station) with the path now crossing wild and windswept cliffs high above the shore. Once past an early 19th-century navigation beacon, known locally as The Daymark, continue along the cliffs by Pepper Hole. A gate above the cliffs leads onto a broad path.

Follow this southwest, enjoying the views to Trevose Head, then drop steeply over a stream and climb to pass through a gap in a wall. Descend away from the craggy backdrop of Porthmissen Bridge to gain a single-track road just before Trevone Bay car park.

Turn left and climb a steep road away from Trevone. Just before a house take a

rough track on the right. Follow this past some farm buildings across scenic countryside, bearing left at a fork on the way to reach a crossroads beside Padstow Farm Shop.

Turn right, then immediately left to cross a stile to the left of a little stone building opposite the shop. Follow a field path (where livestock may be grazing) and cross a stile at the right corner. Walk over another field, again exiting by a stile at its right corner. Turn right and go down a quiet road to the B3276 beside the entrance of Prideaux Place, an Elizabethan manor house and a popular visitor attraction.

Go left onto Church Street and walk back into Padstow at Market Street. Carry straight on to reach the harbour.

◄ The Daymark, Stepper Point

New Polzeath and Rumps Point

Distance 6.5km Time 2 hours
Terrain coastal and clifftop paths
Map OS Explorer 106 **Access** regular buses
from Wadebridge to New Polzeath; car
park in New Polzeath (parking charge)

**The headland of Rumps Point is one
of the most iconic locations along
Cornwall's northern coast. The point has
two distinctive peaks, known as
The Rumps, which strike out into the
Atlantic and are the site of an Iron Age
fort. The rocky island of The Mouls stands
to the northeast of Rumps Point and is an
important breeding ground for puffins
and gannets. An excellent path skirts the
cliffs around Pentire Point and onto The
Rumps before returning to New Polzeath
via Pentire Farm.**

The start point for this walk is the
popular village of New Polzeath. Facing
Hayle Bay on Atlantic Terrace, turn right
and follow the road as it sweeps right to a
public path on the left for Pentire Point.
Drop down around Pentireglaze Haven,
then go through a gate.

The path now climbs steeply, bearing
right up steps before turning left and
descending to a fork. Take the left branch
(right is for Pentire Farm, the return
route) and head northwest along this
rugged stretch of coast. Once through a
gate a gradual climb, to the left of an old
but well-maintained wall, gives views of
New Polzeath and Polzeath and across
Padstow Bay to Stepper Point.

Keep climbing up and over a crest onto
Pentire Point (this simply translates from

Cornish as 'headland') to a wall at
the cliff edge. The views now open
out to the southwest and
Trevose Head. Turn right and
walk northeast, high
above the coast with
the wall to the left.
After passing
through a gap in
the wall you get a
great view of
Rumps Point.

The wall is now on
the right as the path drops
gradually and then climbs
through a gate above Rumps
Point. The view extends across
Port Quin Bay to Kellan Head and
beyond. Continue past a gate for
Pentire Farm and descend onto The
Rumps, where the fort's ditches and
banks are still evident.

This is also a wildlife watcher's dream:
gannet, fulmar, cormorant, shag,
kittiwake, razorbill, guillemot, puffin,
shearwater, petrel, skua and auk, as
well as bottlenose and common dolphin,
porpoise and seals may be spotted at
various times of year.

Retrace your steps to the gate for
Pentire Farm and turn left through this.
Walk across the left edge of two fields and
over a couple of stiles onto a farm track.
This drops down through another gate to
arrive at Pentire Farm. Once opposite the
main farmhouse, beside a small car park,

turn right through a gate, signposted for
the coast, and follow a path down
through a lovely little corridor of
hedgerows, with views of Stepper Point.

Drop down through an attractive
valley to reach the outward-bound path.
Turn left and retrace your steps to New
Polzeath and the start.

◀ Rumps Point

83

Rock to St Enodoc Church

Distance 4km **Time** 1 hour 30
Terrain coastal and hillside paths
Map OS Explorer 106 **Access** bus from
Wadebridge to Rock; ferry from Padstow
to Rock; car park at the west end of Rock
(parking charge)

The village of Rock stands on the east bank
of the Camel Estuary south of Polzeath.
This short walk leaves here for St Enodoc
Church, before climbing Brea Hill for
panoramic views. The rocks used as ballast
by sailing ships which unloaded across the
estuary at Padstow were quarried here and
thought to have given Rock its name. It is
now a haven for yachts and small craft, and
has attracted the attention of the rich, the
royal and the famous.

From the car park, take the path
signposted for St Enodoc Church. When
the path forks, go left as it makes its way
through the dunes above the Camel
Estuary. There are fine views of Padstow
from here.

After dropping down some steps and
crossing a little stream the path forks
again; go left and follow the sandy path
north, with the rounded slopes of Brea Hill
ahead. Keep right at a waymark and
continue to the left of St Enodoc Golf
Course. When nearing a large white house
and copse of trees take the right branch as
the path splits, signposted for the church.

Carefully cross the golf course and carry
straight on at a crossroads. Upon reaching
a narrow road, turn left, then right and at

the next waymark go right across a little bridge. Immediately turn left where the path continues along the left edge of the golf course. Carry on to reach St Enodoc Church, which stands on the edge of the course on the outskirts of Trebetherick. It is a distinctive little building, parts of which date back to the 12th century. From the 16th century much of St Enodoc was beneath the sand dunes before it was renovated in 1864. The writer and former poet laureate Sir John Betjeman is buried in the churchyard.

Continue along the left edge of the course past a green and a tee. Take a waymarked path on the left across a fairway. After another green the path veers right to a crossroads. Go left, then left at the next junction towards Brea Hill and just before the sandy beach of Daymer Bay turn left again to follow a path over a footbridge. Go right onto the beach before bearing left to take the very steep path onto Brea Hill's rounded grassy top.

Its position above the estuary gives great views across Daymer Bay to Polzeath and towards Stepper Point. The summit also holds several Bronze Age tumuli.

Walk over the summit, then drop gradually towards the large white house. At a fence turn right and carry on to reach a sandy path which swings left to a junction. Turn left, and at a fork go left and then right at the next to follow a path through the low-lying dunes.

As you approach Rock turn left at a waymark for a short-lived climb back to the outward path. Turn right and retrace your steps to the start.

Wadebridge and the River Camel

Distance 9.5km **Time** 2 hours 30
Terrain woodland and riverbank paths,
minor roads **Map** OS Explorer 106
Access Wadebridge is well served by public
transport from across Cornwall; several
car parks in Wadebridge (parking charge)

**The River Camel rises on Bodmin Moor
and flows for 50km to Padstow. One of its
loveliest stretches runs through
Wadebridge. Follow good paths and quiet
roads through the countryside before
enjoying a scenic section of the Camel
Trail to complete this loop.**

In 1312 the town of Wade (Old English for
'ford') was designated a market town, with
the suffix of bridge being applied when the
stone bridge that spans the River Camel
was built in the 15th century. The town's
position on the banks of the river was
central to Wadebridge's development over
the centuries, as was the railway when it
arrived in 1834. The now disused railway
line forms the basis of the Camel Trail.

Facing Wadebridge Town Hall on The
Platt, turn left. At a roundabout go left
again onto Jubilee Road and sweep right
onto Southern Way. Follow this past the
John Betjeman Centre onto Guineaport
Road and continue to reach the start of the
Camel Trail beside the River Camel. Do not
join the trail; instead keep straight on to
join a track signposted for Treraven. This
climbs steadily through a gate onto a field
path, which continues through another
gate to reach a woodland path.

At a crossroads turn left to follow a track
which sweeps right into woodland. At a
fork keep right past a house and continue
south through another gate. In due course

◀ Wadebridge and the River Camel

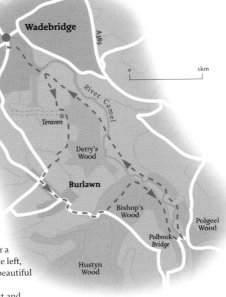

the track veers right; continue to climb gradually and just before another gate turn left, then right. After a gate a minor road is reached beside a large stone house. Go straight on and after 100m turn left at a crossroads into the quiet village of Burlawn.

Walk along the narrow road, soon bearing left and descending steeply through the countryside. Keep an eye out for traffic. Eventually the road veers left past Gamekeepers Cottage and Hustyn Mill. Cross a bridge over a stream, ignore a footpath on the left, and take the next left into the beautiful Bishop's Wood.

A broad track heads northeast and before long swings right to continue alongside the languid River Camel. At a junction go left and carry on, eventually passing around a barrier.

Walk through a car park, then turn left to cross Polbrock Bridge over the River Camel. Bear left through a gate, drop down through another gate and turn left onto the Camel Trail. This runs for nearly 30km between Padstow and Wenford Bridge, utilising a stretch of railway that was once part of the Atlantic Coast Express.

Sightings of kingfisher, heron, geese and otter are all possible along here.

Follow the track northwest alongside the river for around 1.5km to pass what was once the Shooting Range Platform – a halt for hunters on the nearby marshland – and then cross a bridge. With the River Camel now to the right, carry on to enjoy views of Egloshayle and Wadebridge before reaching Guineaport Road. Retrace your steps into Wadebridge.

Port Isaac and Port Quin

Distance 9.5km **Time** 3 hours 30
Terrain coastal paths, some steep ascents
and descents **Map** OS Explorer 106
Access regular buses from Wadebridge to
Port Isaac; there is a car park just off the
B3267 on the outskirts of Port Isaac
(parking charge)

A 5km stretch of beautiful undulating
coastline, which includes a number of
very steep ascents, separates Port Isaac
and Port Quin. Overall the path is good,
although it can be a little slippy on
some of the descents.

Begin the walk from Port Isaac Harbour.
The village has become increasingly
popular in recent years since the television
drama *Doc Martin*, set in the fictional
village of Portwenn, was filmed here.
It has been a fishing village since the
13th century, however, and grew into a
busy coastal port with stone, coal, timber
and pottery exported around the world
from the harbour. Trade continued to
grow during the 19th century when the
railway arrived.

Turn left from the harbour, then right
onto Roscarrock Hill to follow the narrow

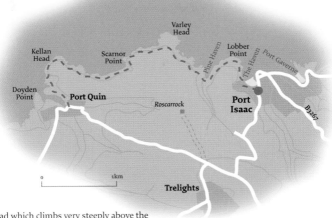

road which climbs very steeply above the village. At the top turn right onto a coastal path, with steps again climbing steeply onto cliffs with views across Port Isaac Bay.

Once above Lobber Point the incline eases and a high-level path traverses the clifftop where cattle may be grazing. In due course a gradual descent brings you through a gate and over a footbridge at Pine Haven.

From here it is a long, tough climb up steps. At the top a well-worn fenced path hugs the indented and steeply undulating coast; black headed gull, kittiwake, Manx shearwater, and shags are visitors to the cliffs here. Once through a gate, a short diversion peels right onto a great vantage point on Varley Head.

To continue the walk carry straight on through another gate as the path heads southwest along the cliff edge. Follow the path as it swings left and climbs to Reedy Cliff. From here you can see what lies ahead as the path wends its way along the coast to Kellan Head with views extending to Rumps Point and The Mouls.

Another steep drop takes you down from Reedy Cliff on steps which zigzag towards the shore. It is then a gradual ascent along a good path to round Kellan Head. As you head towards Port Quin the cliff-edge folly of Doyden Castle can be seen across the bay at Doyden Point. Dating from 1830, it was built by local businessman Samuel Symons as a retreat to host decadent gambling parties.

Carry on along the path, passing through a few gates to reach the small hamlet of Port Quin, where there are only a few houses and a slipway. This is a lovely quiet place for a break before retracing your steps along the clifftop to Port Isaac.

◀ Kellan Head

Crackington Haven to Cambeak

Distance 3km **Time** 1 hour 15
Terrain coastal paths, some steep ascents
and descents **Map** OS Explorer 126
Access regular buses from Wadebridge
and Bude to Crackington Haven; car park
in Crackington (parking charges)

Although this is a short walk, there are
several steep ascents – particularly the
climb onto Cambeak – that make it quite
tough. However, Crackington Haven is
a lovely little spot with a good pub and
café, interesting geology and some
stunning views.

The cove of Crackington Haven nestles
between the angular slopes of Cambeak
and the steep-sided cliffs of Pencannow

Point. Its name derives from the Cornish
word *crak*, meaning 'sandstone', which
relates to the distinctive geology to be
found here.

There is also a wide variety of wildlife to
be spotted during this walk – out to sea
there may be grey seals (and if you're very
fortunate bottlenose dolphins and
basking shark), whilst around the paths
linnet, skylark, stonechat, kestrel and
many species of butterfly, including red
admiral and small pearl-bordered
fritillary, are often seen.

From the car park, turn left and cross a
bridge before going right along a stony
track which veers left through a gate.
Head past the tennis courts and through

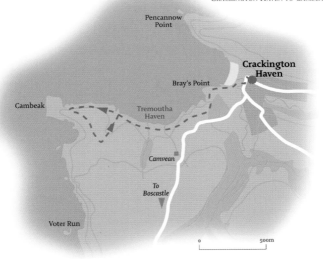

another gate to reach a fork. Take the right branch and when it forks again go left. A steeper climb offers great views across the beach to Pencannow Point's vertical cliffs.

Once down some steps the fin-like shape of Cambeak dominates the view. Beyond a gate a steep flight of steps drops towards the shore. The wildflower-lined path soon passes through several more gates and crosses two footbridges before a steep pull takes you above the coast again and then drops down over a stile. After another footbridge the path splits.

Take the right branch for a steep climb onto the summit of Cambeak and a far-reaching view which stretches north along Bude Bay and south along the great

cliffs of North Cornwall, including High Cliff which, at 225m, is Cornwall's highest. But it is the geology that really impresses – the rock here has been folded and bent into shape over the last 350 million years and the interbedded sandstone and shale has become known as the Crackington Formation. The best example of it can be seen in the cliffs a little beneath the summit.

From the top it is a steep descent southeast to reach a waymarked path on the left. This drops gradually down through Cam Dean, contouring the lower slopes of Cambeak. When you reach a fork turn right to return to the path followed earlier. Cross the footbridge and retrace your steps, with a couple of steep climbs, to Crackington Haven.

◀ Crackington Haven from Cambeak

Northcott Mouth from Bude

Distance 5.25km **Time** 1 hour 30
Terrain coastal and countryside paths,
pavement **Map** OS Explorer 126
Access regular buses from Wadebridge
and Launceston to Bude; several car parks
in Bude (parking charges)

**This is a short, simple walk that leaves
from the busy seaside resort of Bude and
follows field tracks to Northcott Mouth, a
great spot to sit and enjoy the beach and
surf. Follow a scenic stretch of coastal
path to return to Bude.**

Well-known today for its surfing, Bude
sits at the mouth of the River Neet and has
been a popular tourist destination since
Victorian times – many of the distinctive

buildings in the town date from this time,
as well as from the Edwardian and
Georgian periods. The Bude Canal also
reaches its journey's end here; it was
opened in 1825 to transport the mineral-
rich sand to farms in North Cornwall,
running as far as Launceston.

From Summerleaze car park follow the
access road onto Granville Terrace. At a
junction turn left onto Belle Vue Road and
climb through the town, passing the
striking white post office building. When
the road splits keep left onto Crooklets
Road, which descends alongside a golf
course, with expansive views across the
surrounding countryside.

Once past Crooklets car park the road

sweeps right. Just before a bridge turn left, then left again onto Maer Down Road (signposted as a public bridleway). Climb gradually past several houses to the top of the road, then go through a gate onto a rough track. This continues north, crossing a field, where stonechat, fieldfare and several types of butterfly may be seen amongst the hedgerows in summer, to pass through a gate beside a distinctive white cottage.

After a short section of rough road turn left, just before a junction, onto a path and descend to Northcott Mouth, a beautiful little beach, framed by steep cliffs and popular with surfers. There are several interesting geological formations here and at low tide the remains of *SS Belem*, a Portuguese steamship which ran aground in 1917, are revealed.

Turn left for a short steady climb away from the beach. Keep left at a fork and return to the white cottage passed on the outward route. Once through the gate peel right to leave the track followed earlier and keep to this grassy path as it climbs gently along Maer Cliff.

Great views again extend north along Bude Bay and south to Bude Haven's

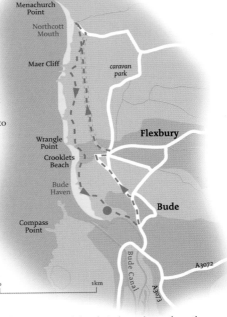

sandy beach. As it continues, the path passes through a couple of gates and onto a rough track, which drops down to Bude Haven.

Walk through a small car park, but just before a road turn right down steps onto a paved path. Cross a footbridge over a stream, then walk above Bude Haven, passing above the old tidal swimming pool. Soon the path swings left to reach a café on the right. Drop down steps here to a road, go left and walk back to the car park at the start.

◄ Northcott Mouth

Morwenstow and Duckpool

Distance 11.25km **Time** 3 hours 45
Terrain coastal paths, woodland paths,
minor roads **Map** OS Explorer 126
Access limited bus service from Bude to
Morwenstow; free car park at Morwenstow

The scattering of houses at Morwenstow,
near Cornwall's northern extremity, is
the starting point for this tough clifftop
walk. There are several steep ascents and
descents along this route where some
cliffs rise to more than 120m in height.

Begin from the small car park facing the
Rectory Tearoom, which resides in a 13th-
century farmhouse. Turn right, follow a
track through a gate onto a field-edge
path and past the 12th-century church.
Between 1834 and 1874 the vicar was the
eccentric Reverend Robert Stephen
Hawker. He built his rectory below the
church in a Victorian Gothic style.

Continue through several gates to
reach cliffs high above the serrated
coastline. Once through a gate signposted
for 'Hawker's Hut' walk southwest along
the right edge of a field and through a
gate to a flight of steps on the right. These
drop down to a simple driftwood hut
built into the cliffs where the Reverend
was inspired to write much of his poetry,
including 'The Song of the Western Men',
Cornwall's National Anthem.

Keep south along the path. It soon
drops sharply to cross a footbridge, then
climbs steeply onto Higher Sharpnose
Point. Keep left past an old lookout
station. After another steep descent, walk
right at a junction, cross another bridge,

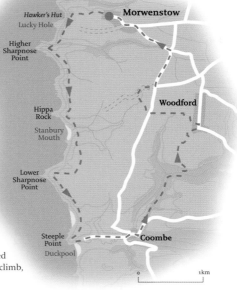

turn left and climb steeply through a gate to pass the GCHQ radio tracking station.

Here the path widens onto an old access road, but bear right from it back to the coast. Once through a gate and over a stile the path crosses the thin wedge of Steeple Point, then swings left to drop down into Duckpool.

Follow a road east through a wooded valley. Turn left at a junction, then right and go across a bridge over a ford. Sweep left along the road past several thatched cottages and, as it begins to climb, bear left onto a waymarked woodland path.

Follow this for just over 1km, then turn left to cross a waymarked stile. Cross a bridge over a stream, then a track. Turn right onto the next track and ascend steeply to a junction. Go left and climb out of the woodland where there are great views across Coombe Valley. Beyond a gate follow a field edge to a road at Woodford. Turn left, go down past several houses, then turn left at a junction.

After 50m follow a footpath on the left between cottages through a gate. Turn right, then left and follow a field edge which sweeps right to cross a stile on the left. Cross another field, go over two stiles, bear left and diagonally cross a field to a pocket of woodland at Eastaway Manor. After another stile, a path passes houses to reach a minor road.

Cross this through a gate, turn right, then left and follow the field edge around to the right. Turn left through a gate to Stanbury Farm. Go right, then right again onto a minor road. At a crossroads turn left and continue through the countryside for 1.25km into Crosstown. Keep left and walk past the 13th-century Bush Inn back to the start.

◀ Clifftop above 'Hawker's Hut'

Index